CL00705406

1 MONTH OF
FREE
READING

at

www.ForgottenBooks.com

By purchasing this book you are eligible for one month membership to ForgottenBooks.com, giving you unlimited access to our entire collection of over 1,000,000 titles via our web site and mobile apps.

To claim your free month visit:

www.forgottenbooks.com/free196795

* Offer is valid for 45 days from date of purchase. Terms and conditions apply.

ISBN 978-0-266-19690-7
PIBN 10196795

This book is a reproduction of an important historical work. Forgotten Books uses
state-of-the-art technology to digitally reconstruct the work, preserving the original format
whilst repairing imperfections present in the aged copy. In rare cases, an imperfection in
the original, such as a blemish or missing page, may be replicated in our edition. We do,
however, repair the vast majority of imperfections successfully; any imperfections that
remain are intentionally left to preserve the state of such historical works.

Forgotten Books is a registered trademark of FB &c Ltd.
Copyright © 2018 FB &c Ltd.
FB &c Ltd, Dalton House, 60 Windsor Avenue, London, SW19 2RR.
Company number 08720141. Registered in England and Wales.

For support please visit www.forgottenbooks.com

MINUTES

OF THE

PROCEEDINGS

OF THE

SECOND CONVENTION OF DELEGATES

OF THE

BRITISH AMERICAN LEAGUE,

Held at Toronto, C. W., on Thursday, November 1, and by Adjournment on the 2nd, 3rd, 5th, 6th and 7th of November, 1849.

———

TORONTO:

PRINTED AT THE PATRIOT OFFICE, YONGE STREET.

1849.

MINUTES

OF THE

PROCEEDINGS

OF THE

SECOND CONVENTION OF DELE

MEMBERS PRESENT :

Aikman, Michael	Barton.	Hatt, John O.	Hamilton.
Armstrong, Arthur	Lloydtown.	Holly, Joseph	Weston.
Armstrong, Thomas	Beckwith.	Kenny, Robert	Ottawa County.
Balfour, John	Kitley.	Langton, John	Peterborough.
Bartles, James F.	Richmond Towns'p	Lemon, Charles	Escott.
Benjamin, George	Belleville.	Lewis, Daniel	Saltfleet.
Bottom, W. H.	Oxford.	MacKechnie, S. E.	Newcastle District.
Boggs, G. W.	St. Thomas.	Moffatt, Hon. George	Montreal.
Boulton, D'Arcy E.	Newcastle District.	Mack, William G.	Montreal.
Bowes, J. G.	Toronto.	McDonald, Rolland	St. Catherines.
Bridgeford, David	Thornhill & Richmond Hill.	McBean, Arthur	Newcastle.
		Merigold, Charles	Brantford.
Boswell, John C.	Newcastle District.	Miller, D. G.	Huron.
Brooke, George	Kitley.	Muttlebury, J. W.	Elizabethtown.
Boyer, George	Newcastle.	Mair, Thomas	Yonge.
Burnham, Asa A.	Newcastle District.	Macdonald, W. S.	Leeds & Lansdowne
Carroll, Peter	Flamboro' East.	Merwin, J. S.	Lansdowne.
Campbell, Francis	Chinguacousy.	McKinnon, John	Bytown.
Crawford, John	Lansdowne.	McLean, Alexander	Cornwall Towns'p.
Carr, John	Yonge.	Macdonell, A. J.	Kingston Towns'p.
Crawford, George	Brockville.	McKay, William	Nelson.
Cockburn, James	Newcastle District.	Murney, Edmund	Belleville.
Covernton, James	Charlotteville.	Neale, Francis	York Mills.
Coverntown, C. W.	Woodhouse.	O'Brien, E. G.	Escott.
Deykes, Thomas	Kingston.	Pass, Archibald, M.D.	Simcoe District.
Darby, James	St. Thomas.	Patton, James	Simcoe District.
Duggan, John	Scarborough.	Parsons, Albert	Wolford.
Denison, George T. jr.	Beckwith.	Playfair, Colonel	Perth.
Deedes, Edmund	Oxford County.	Pringle, Jacob F.	Cornwall Towns'p.
Davis, William	Yonge.	Pirie, George	Guelph.
Dempsey, Richard	North Crosby.	Raines, J. R.	Trafalgar.
Douglas, John	Oxford.	Read, D. B.	Wolford.
Dixon, Thomas C.	London.	Reynolds, John	Johnstown District.
Duggan, George, jr.	Toronto.	Robinson, A. G.	Orillia.
Forsyth, John R.	Kingston.	Rowlands, Samuel	Kingston Towns'p.
Fraser, Colonel	Perth.	Scobie, Hugh	Toronto.
French, John S.	Oxford, Johns. Dis.	Smillie, R. R.	Hamilton.
Ferres, J. M.	South Crosby.	Smith, James	Toronto Township.
Ford, D. B. O.	Brockville.	Strachan, John	Huron.
Gamble, J. W.	Vaughan.	Switzer, B.	Toronto Township.
Gurney, E. T. P.	Grimsby.	Stone, Lyman	Gower.
Gamble, Wm.	Etobicoke.	Stabback, James	Whitby.
Gowan, O. R.	Elizabethtown.	Thompson, Samuel	Burgess.
Glassford, Paul	Yonge.	Vankoughnet, P. M.	Toronto.
Hamilton, A. C.	Grantham.	Vansittart, J. G.	Oxford.
Hamilton, J., M. D.	Beverly & Flambro	Wilson, Thomas	Quebec.
Harris, T. S.	Trafalgar.	Young, Wm.	Hillier.
Harvey, Robert	Augusta.	Young, John	Hamilton.
Hooker, Alfred	Augusta.		

MINUTES, &c.

The Convention met.

The Hon. George Moffatt, Chairman, having taken his seat, read the resolution of last session, providing for future meetings of the Convention, and also the notice of the Central Committee, by virtue of which the convention was now assembled.

Mr. J. W. Gamble gave notice that he would, on to-morrow, move that it be resolved—

1. That the condition of this province calls loudly upon all lovers of peace and good government, speedily to adopt measures whereby the present excitement may be allayed, public tranquillity restored, and existing political differences merged in one paramount sentiment—the good of our common country. Since the burning of the parliament houses, disturbance has followed disturbance, and riot has succeeded riot in quick succession; on several occasions human blood has been shed, the law violated with impunity, while the government, by their ineffectual attempts to repress these disorders, have been brought into contempt. Exciting and irritating political questions, involving the dismemberment of this colony from the empire, are openly advocated, engendering discontent, discord, and fierce political animosities. Rancorous feelings are separating neighbour from neighbour, to the hindrance and neglect of business, the interruption of industry, the loss of confidence, and the destruction of credit. The public mind is becoming vitiated by these excesses, a spirit of insubordination to the laws is manifested, which, if allowed to prevail, threatens to burst asunder the bonds of society, and lead to the most deplorable consequences—anarchy, confusion and civil strife.

2. That in order to assuage the present excitement and discontent, to prevent collision between our fellow subjects, to promote union among all, and to determine the great political questions now

agitating the public mind, in accordance with public opinion, it is necessary that the feelings, sentiments and opinions of the people, should be faithfully represented in the Legislative Assembly, at its next session; which can only be attained by the exercise of the royal prerogative, in the dissolution of the present parliament and the summoning of a new one.

3. That while the three remedial measures, Protection, Retrenchment and Union, held forth by the British American League, are manifestly those best calculated to effect the desired change and restore prosperity to our drooping interests, it is equally apparent that those measures cannot be carried into successful operation, the necessary reforms accomplished, and a just, wise and cheap system of government established, without important alterations in our constitution, requiring joint and concerted action with our sister provinces. To this end it is expedient to obtain the authority of the legislature, for holding a General Convention of Delegates, for the purpose of considering and preparing, in concert with delegates from those provinces, a new constitution, to be afterwards submitted for ratification to the people of Canada, and of such of the other colonies as may decide upon acting in unison with them, preparatory to its being brought under the consideration of the metropolitan government.

Mr. GOWAN gave notice that he would, on to-morrow, move that it be resolved—

1. That these colonies cannot continue in their present political or commercial state.

2. That the evils by which they are oppressed have had their origin in the withdrawal of protection, by the mother country; and in the vicious and improvident administration of their affairs, by the local government.

3. That by Great Britain returning to her former protective policy of " Ships, Colonies and Commerce ;" or by causing to be opened to the trade and commerce of these colonies the markets of foreign countries, and especially of the United States of America, upon terms of a fair and honourable reciprocity; united to the reduction of the expenses of the civil government to the lowest scale, consistent with the efficiency of the public service, and a vigorous, honest and impartial administration of the government, untrammelled by the ties of faction, peace and prosperity may yet be restored to the country.

4. That if the interests of the British people will not admit of protection to colonial products in her market, and if she will not, or cannot, open the markets of foreign countries, and especially of the United States of America, for the admission of colonial products and manufactures, on terms of reciprocity, then will it become the duty of colonists to create at home, or to seek abroad, a market or markets for the products of their own industry; and thus, by following the

example of the mother country, seek the welfare of their own people, irrespective of British interests or British influences.

5. That a committee of five members be now chosen, to draft a petition to the Queen, and both houses of the Imperial Parliament, based upon the foregoing resolutions; and that a deputation of two gentlemen be chosen, to proceed to England, to lay the final appeal, for justice to British America, at the foot of the throne.

6. That, pending the decision of England, our fellow-colonists of all classes be earnestly entreated to abstain from subscribing declarations, calling for a severance of the political relations which bind us to the mother country—that they be respectfully invited to abide in patience the result—that if driven to a dissolution of the ties, hitherto held sacred, the responsibility, the onus and the odium of the act, may rest with England, not with Canada; and that posterity may judge our conduct as that of a suffering and insulted people, who had exhausted every honourable means to ward off a separation, which they could not contemplate without sorrow, and could not sanction, except as a last resort.

7. That whether protection or reciprocity shall be conceded or withheld, it is essential to the contentment of the country, and to its future good government, that a constitution should be framed in unison with the wishes of the people, and suited to the growing greatness and intelligence of the country; and that as much diversity of opinion exists, and must continue to exist, upon a subject so important, it is desirable that a convention of the people, without distinction of party, should be legalized by act of parliament, to draft a constitution for the province, to be submitted to the Imperial Parliament for its concurrence and adoption.

8. That the best thanks of the convention be respectfully presented to the Hon. Charles Symons and to the Hon. John Robertson, of New Brunswick, for the zeal and patriotism they manifested in visiting Canada, and for the talent and discretion which marked their conduct, during their recent conference with the committee of gentlemen named by this convention, during its late session at Kingston.

Mr. JOHN DUGGAN moved, seconded by Mr. ROLLAND MAC-DONALD,

That Samuel Thompson, Benjamin Switzer, and Arthur Armstrong, Esquires, be a committee of finance during the present session of this Convention.—Which was carried.

Dr. JAMES HAMILTON moved, seconded by Mr. WILSON,

That one hundred and fifty copies of the resolutions submitted by Mr. Gamble, of Vaughan, be printed for the use of members of the Convention.—Which was carried.

Mr. AIKMAN moved, seconded by Mr. SWITZER,

That one hundred and fifty copies of the resolutions proposed by

Mr. GOWAN be printed for the use of members.—Which was carried.

The Convention adjourned until to-morrow, at ten o'clock, a. m.

FRIDAY, Nov. 2, 1849.

The Convention met, pursuant to adjournment, at ten o'clock, a. m.

Mr. WILSON brought up the report of the Committee of Conference on the Union of the Provinces, which was read as follows:—

Report of progress of " Committee of Conference," on the Union of the British American Provinces.

In obedience to the resolution passed by the convention of the "British American League," when in session at Kingston in July last, the Committee of Conference, then and there appointed, have to report as follows:

That considerable delay was experienced in preparing and publishing the information it was deemed necessary to lay before the colonists of the Lower Provinces, owing to untoward and accidental circumstances.

That there being no associations, known to your committee, organized in Nova Scotia, Prince Edward's Island and Newfoundland, a communication was made to "prominent and influential" parties in Halifax, requesting them to co-operate with your Committee by disseminating, through Nova Scotia, Prince Edward's Island and Newfoundland, the printed proceedings of the Convenvention, accompanied by circulars, written for the purpose of inviting the action of those provinces on a proposition for a union of all the colonies.

That your Committee communicated similarly to the " Colonial Association of New Brunswick," which society responded by appointing the Hon. Charles Simonds and the Hon. John Robertson to the Conference. These gentlemen were not however authorised to act definitively, but only to ascertain the views and opinions of the " British American League," and report thereon on their return.

That the following members of your Committee met the Hon. Charles Simonds and the Hon. John Robertson in conference in Montreal, on the 13th and 14th instant, viz. Messrs. J. W. Gamble, George Crawford, O. R. Gowan, H. C. Montgomerie, and Thomas Wilson.

That the following is a copy of the minute then and there made, as expressing the opinion of this Conference, arrived at after a close and thoughtful discussion of the question proposed for consideration :

" At a meeting held at Montreal, on the 13th of October, 1849— Present—Hon. Charles Simonds, Hon. John Robertson of New

Brunswick, Messrs. O. R. Gowan, George Crawford, Thomas Wilson, H. E. Montgomerie and J. W. Gamble of Canada.

"In the course of conversation and discussion, it was elicited as the unanimous opinion of those present—

"That the commercial evils now oppressing the British American Colonies, are to be traced principally to the abandonment by Great Britain of her former colonial policy, thus depriving them of the preference previously enjoyed in the British market, without securing any equivalent advantages in any other market.

"That these colonies cannot remain in their present position without the prospect of immediate ruin, and that it is the duty of the Imperial Government either—First, to restore to the colonies a preference in the British markets over foreign countries—or second, to cause to be opened to them the markets of foreign countries, and more especially the United States, upon terms of reciprocity,—one or other of which is considered indispensable to the continuance of our present political connection with Great Britain.

"That a Union of the British American Provinces, on mutually advantageous and finally arranged terms, with the concession from the mother country of enlarged powers of self-government (including the unrestricted privilege of making laws to regulate and protect their commercial and industrial interests, and to reduce the expenditure of the civil government to an adequate scale) appears essential to the prosperity of the provinces.

"That deputations from the 'British American League,' and 'New Brunswick Colonial Association' should meet at Halifax at as early a day as possible, with such gentlemen from the other provinces as may attend, for the purpose of arranging a definite scheme of union to submit for public approval."

Your Committee then adjourned, upon a proposition to meet again in Halifax, in the hope that they would be there met by representatives from Nova Scotia, Prince Edward's Island and Newfoundland, for the further consideration of the proposed union of the provinces.

THOMAS WILSON, *Chairman, Comm. Conference.*

Toronto, Oct. 31, 1849.

Mr. DEYKES moved, seconded by Mr. W. S. MACDONALD,

That the report just read be laid upon the table.—Which was carried.

Mr. WILSON gave notice that he would move the following resolutions:

1. That having due regard to the public interests, the promotion of industry, and the stability of the value of property, it is essential to establish in this colony a "Provincial Bank of Issue," to give to

the country a circulating medium, and that such circulating medium should not be convertible into specie, on demand.

2. That to bring into free and fructifying use the dispersed unemployed capital throughout the province, and give profitable activity to manufactures and agriculture, it is necessary to establish a general banking law, granting power to parties to incorporate themselves for banking purposes, under such restrictions only as may be necessary to guard the public from imposition, loss and injury.

3. That regarding the good of the people as the foundation of all government, this convention considers the mode of constituting that of this colony as most objectionable, unjust and injurious, and that to effect the necessary change, to enable a salutary power, commanding the confidence and respect of the people, the members of the Legislative Council and the Governor General should be elected.

Mr. J. W. GAMBLE moved, seconded by Mr. McKINNON,

That it be resolved, That the condition of this province calls loudly upon all lovers of peace and good government speedily to adopt measures whereby the present excitement may be allayed, public tranquillity restored, and existing political differences merged in one paramount sentiment—the good of our common country. Since the burning of the parliament houses, disturbance has followed disturbance, and riot has succeeded riot, in quick succession; on several occasions human blood has been shed, the law violated with impunity, while the government, by their ineffectual attempts to repress these disorders, have been brought into contempt. Exciting and irritating political questions, involving the dismemberment of this colony from the empire, are openly advocated, engendering discontent, discord, and fierce political animosities; rancorous feelings are separating neighbour from neighbour, to the hindrance and neglect of business, the interruption of industry, the loss of confidence, and the destruction of credit; the public mind is becoming vitiated by these excesses, a spirit of insubordination to the laws is manifested, which, if allowed to prevail, threatens to burst asunder the bonds of society, and lead to the most deplorable consequences—anarchy, confusion and civil strife.

Mr. AIKMAN moved in amendment, seconded by Mr. A. J. MACDONELL, to strike out that part of the resolution beginning at the words, "since the burning of the Parliament Houses," and ending at the word "contempt."—Which was lost.

Mr. R. MACDONALD moved in amendment, seconded by Mr. JOHN STRACHAN,

That the words "burning of the parliament houses," in the original resolution, be expunged, and that the words "passing of the Rebellion Losses Bill," be inserted in their stead.—Which was lost.

Mr. CRAWFORD moved in amendment, seconded by Mr. W. S. MACDONALD.

That the resolution be not adopted, but that the following be substituted :

Resolved, That the condition of this province calls loudly upon all lovers of peace and good government speedily to adopt measures whereby the excitement now generally pervading the colony may be removed, public tranquillity restored, and existing political differences merged in one paramount sentiment — the good of our common country.

Which amendment, being put to the vote, was lost.

Mr. GOWAN moved in amendment, seconded by Mr. LANGTON,

That the words " since the burning of the parliament houses," be struck out of the original motion, and the words " for some time past," be substituted in lieu thereof.—Which was carried.

Mr. CRAWFORD moved in amendment, seconded by Mr. W. S. MACDONALD,

That the words " engendering discontent, discord, and fierce political animosities," be struck out.—Which was lost.

Mr. GOWAN moved in amendment, seconded by Mr. MURNEY,

That these colonies cannot continue in their present political or commercial state.

The convention then adjourned till seven o'clock, p. m.

————

The convention having met pursuant to adjournment,

Mr. GOWAN asked for and obtained leave to withdraw his amendment to Mr. J. W. Gamble's resolution.

Mr. J. W. GAMBLE asked for and obtained leave to withdraw his resolution.

Mr. J. W. GAMBLE then moved, seconded by Mr. GOWAN,

That it be resolved, That the condition of this province calls loudly upon all lovers of peace and good government, speedily to adopt measures whereby the present excitement may be allayed, public tranquillity restored, and existing political differences merged in one paramount sentiment—the good of our common country. For some time past, disturbance has followed disturbance, and riot has succeeded riot in quick succession ; on several occasions human blood has been shed, the law violated with impunity, while the government, by their ineffectual attempts to repress these disorders, have been brought into contempt ; exciting and irritating political questions, involving the dismemberment of this colony from the empire, are openly advocated ; rancorous feelings are separating neighbour from neighbour, to the hindrance and neglect of business, the interruption of industry, the loss of confidence, and the destruction of credit. The public mind is becoming vitiated by these excesses, a spirit of insubordination to the laws is manifested, which, if allowed to prevail, threatens to burst asunder the bonds of society, and lead to the most deplorable consequences—anarchy, confusion, and civil strife; and that for these and other causes, it is the opinion of this convention that these colonies cannot continue in their present political or commercial state.—Which was carried.

Mr. J. W. GAMBLE moved, seconded by Mr. WILSON,

That it be resolved, That in order to assuage the present excitement and discontent, to prevent collision between our fellow subjects, to promote union among all, and to determine the great political questions now agitating the public mind, in accordance with public opinion, it is necessary that the feelings, sentiments, and opinions of the people should be faithfully represented in the Legislative Assembly, at its next session; which can only be attained by the exercise of the royal prerogative in the dissolution of the present parliament and the summoning of a new one.

After some discussion, Mr. GAMBLE asked for and obtained leave to withdraw his motion.

The convention then adjourned until to-morrow, at ten o'clock.

————

SATURDAY, NOVEMBER 3, 1849.

The convention met pursuant to adjournment.

Mr. J. W. GAMBLE moved, seconded by Mr. JOHN YOUNG,

That it be resolved, That while the three remedial measures, protection, retrenchment and union, held forth by the British American League, are manifestly those best calculated to effect the desired change, and restore prosperity to our drooping interests, it is equally apparent that those measures cannot be carried into successful operation, the necessary reforms accomplished, and a just, wise and cheap system of government established, without important alterations in our constitution, requiring joint and concerted action with our sister provinces. To this end it is expedient to obtain the authority of the legislature, for holding a general convention of delegates, for the purpose of considering and preparing, in concert with delegates from those provinces, a new constitution, to be afterwards submitted for ratification to the people of Canada, and of such of the other colonies as may decide upon acting in unison with them, preparatory to its being brought under the consideration of the metropolitan government.

Mr. DIXON moved in amendment, seconded by Mr. E. G. O'BRIEN,

That all after the words " our sister provinces," be struck out, and the following substituted:

To this end it is expedient for this convention to lay down the principles of a constitution for the said union, and submit it to the people of Canada and the other British provinces, and through their

representatives to the imperial government, for confirmation.—
Which was carried.

The resolution, as amended, was then put and carried.

Mr. FORSYTH moved, seconded by Mr. McKINNON,

That the report of the Committee of Conference on the Union of
the Provinces be now taken into consideration.

Mr. J. DUGGAN moved in amendment, seconded by Mr. HAMILTON,

That the delegates appointed at the last session of this convention
be a committee to consider and report on the principles on which a
union of the British American provinces shall take place.—Which
was lost.

The main motion was then put and carried.

Mr. LANGTON moved, seconded by Mr. A. ARMSTRONG,

That the report of the Committee appointed to confer with Delegates from the Lower Provinces be referred to a committee of the
whole, forthwith.—Which was carried.

The convention accordingly resolved itself into the said committee.

Mr. AIKMAN took the chair of the said committee, and, after
some time spent therein, reported that the committee had adopted
the said report.

The Chairman then put the question, whether the said report
should be received.—Which was carried, and the report was ordered
to lie on the table.

Mr. WILSON moved, seconded by Mr. J. DUGGAN,

That it be resolved, That, whether protection or reciprocity shall
be conceded or withheld, it is essential to the welfare of this colony
and its future good government, that a constitution should be framed
in unison with the wishes of the people, and suited to the growing
importance and intelligence of the country, and that such constitution
should embrace a union of the British American provinces, on
mutually advantageous and fairly arranged terms, with the concession from the mother country of enlarged powers of self-government.

Mr. O'BRIEN moved in amendment, seconded by Colonel PLAY-
FAIR,

That the further discussion of these resolutions be postponed,
and that they be printed for the use of members.—Which was lost.

The main motion was then put and carried.

Mr. WILSON moved, seconded by Mr. GOWAN,

That it be resolved, That under the altered commercial policy of
Great Britain, by which the differential duties in favour of colonial
produce have been largely repealed, and the agricultural and commercial interests of British dependencies subjected to the severest
competition in her markets, with foreign rivals independent in their
legislative action, it is obviously unjust to perpetuate the imperial
power to interfere with the proceedings of the colonial government,
adopted to foster and advance our social and industrial welfare.

Mr. O'BRIEN moved in amendment, seconded by Mr. DIXON,

That the resolution be not adopted, but that the following be substituted in lieu thereof:

That while it is our great ambition to build up in the British provinces of North America, a British people, actuated by those high moral and religious principles combined with that spirit of integrity and freedom which has raised Great Britain to the highest station among the nations of the world, it is also our duty both to create at home, and to seek abroad, a market for the products of our own industry. And if the supposed interests of Great Britain will not admit of protection to colonial products in her market; and if she will not, or cannot open the markets of foreign countries, and especially of the United States of America, for the admission of colonial products and manufactures, we shall of necessity be driven by a continuation of the present policy of the mother country to seek the welfare of our own people irrespectively of her interests, or her influences.—Which was lost.

Mr BENJAMIN moved in amendment, seconded by Mr. MILLER,

That the resolution be not adopted, but that the following be substituted in lieu thereof:—

That if the interests of the British people will not admit of protection to colonial products in the markets of Great Britain, then will it become not merely the duty, but the inevitable necessity, of colonists to create at home, or to seek abroad, a market or markets for the products of their own industry; and thus by following the example of the mother country, seek the welfare of their own people, having in view not only the immediate prosperity, but the future prospects of this our country. That in order to enable us to regulate these markets to our own advantage, and for our own safety, it is necessary that we should obtain from Great Britain the controul of the River and Gulph of Saint Lawrence, and the power of imposing as we please, imposts upon British or foreign goods, entering our markets.—Which was lost.

The main motion was then put, and carried.

Mr. MILLER gave notice, that he would move, that it be resolved,

That it is a matter of regret to this Convention, that the subject of a separation of this colony from the mother country and annexation to the United States of America, has been openly advocated by a portion of the press, and of the inhabitants of this province; and this Convention unhesitatingly records its entire disapprobation of this course, and calls upon all well-wishers of their country, to discountenance it by every means in their power.

The Convention then adjourned until Monday next, at ten o'clock, a. m.

MONDAY, NOV. 5, 1849.

The Convention met pursuant to adjournment.

Mr. W. GAMBLE moved, seconded by Mr. THOMPSON,

That it be resolved, that a committee of five members be appointed to enquire and report what amendments to the constitution of the League, and appointments to the Central Committee, have become necessary in consequence of the removal of the seat of government from Montreal to Toronto, and that the Messrs. Gamble, Mack, Forsyth, Rowlands and O'Brien compose the same.—Which was carried.

Mr. AIKMAN moved, seconded by Mr. MUTTLEBURY,

That it be resolved, that the quorum be reduced to twenty members, for the remainder of the present session of the Convention.— Which was carried.

Mr. STRACHAN gave notice, that he will, on to-morrow, move for the appointment of a committee to carry out the following resolution :

That while the three remedial measures, Protection, Retrenchment and Union, held forth by the British American League, are manifestly those best calculated to effect the desired change, and restore prosperity to our drooping interests, it is equally apparent that those measures cannot be carried into successful operation, the necessary reforms accomplished, and a just, wise and cheap system of government established, without important alterations in the constitution, requiring joint and concerted action with our sister provinces—to this end it is expedient for this Convention to lay down the principles of a constitution for the said union, and submit it to the people of Canada and the other British provinces, and through their representatives to the Imperial government for confirmation ; and that he will at the same time humbly submit to this Convention, a sketch of a constitution for British North America, to be laid before the committee, if appointed, for its consideration.

Mr. BOULTON gave notice, that it is his intention to move a series of resolutions, bringing the subject of the public debt of this province before the mother country.

Mr. WILSON moved, seconded by Mr. FORSYTH,

That it be resolved, That regarding the good of the people as the object of all government, and recent events having proved to this Convention, that the present mode of constituting the Legislative Council is dangerous to its independence, and contemplating a union of the British American provinces, it is the opinion of this convention that this branch of the government should be elected.

Mr. MURNEY moved in amendment, seconded by Mr. YOUNG, of Hillier,

That the resolution be not adopted; but that the following be substituted in lieu thereof:

That it is inexpedient for this convention to recommend to the people of Canada any change in the present constitution of this colony. That in addition to its former address, a further declaration be made public of its disapproval of the Montreal manifesto in favor of annexation of this province to the United States, and of its determination to agitate those questions already before the public, which, in the opinion of this convention, will ameliorate our condition, without endangering the connection with the mother country.—— Which was lost.

Mr. BENJAMIN moved in amendment, seconded by Mr. A. J. MACDONELL,

That the resolution be not adopted, but that the following be substituted in lieu thereof:

That it is the opinion of the convention, that it is most essential to provide for the independence of the upper house or legislative council, and to guard against any possibility of an infringement of its privileges by the other branches of the legislature, as well as to avoid the system of packing the legislative council by partizan appointments, which has a direct tendency to deprive that branch of the legislature of that independence which the Constitutional Act contemplated it should enjoy, and that in order to remedy the defect in that body, as at present constituted, it is advisable that the number of its members should be limited to and constantly maintained at half the number of the members of the legislative assembly.— Which was carried.

The resolution, as amended, was then put and carried.

The convention then adjourned until to-morrow, at ten o'clock, a.m.

TUESDAY, NOVEMBER 6, 1849.

The convention met, pursuant to adjournment.

Mr. MACK brought up an address of the Glasgow Reciprocity Association, together with the letters of the convener and secretary accompanying the same.

Mr. HAMILTON moved, seconded by Mr. AIKMAN,

That the communications just read be recorded on the minutes of this convention.—Which was carried.

(Copy.)

GLASGOW, 24th August, 1849.

SIR,—I beg to hand you a copy of an address to the British American League, from the Glasgow Reciprocity and Industrial Association.

The address has been signed by office bearers and members of committee, on behalf of the Association, but is delayed till next mail in order that leading houses and the public generally may have an opportunity of recording their sympathy with the colonies.

I am, Sir,

Your most obedient servant,

HUGH TENNENT, Convener.

The Hon. George Moffatt, Montreal.

(Copy.)

GLASGOW, *24th Aug.*, 1849.

SIR,—I beg to refer to the preceding letter from the convener of the " Glasgow Reciprocity and Industrial Association." I hope to be able to send the document by next mail.

Since this address was published, the address of your league has reached this country, and been reprinted in the papers. It is calculated to do much good, by informing the British public of grievances, of which they have hitherto been kept somewhat in the dark.

Permit me to remark that, although at one time the present Government professed to seek for *reciprocity* with foreign states, the organs of the ministry have, for six months past, *repudiated* the idea of " *reciprocal trade,*" advocating what are called the " *Manchester School* " principles of duty-free imports, purchasing in the cheapest market, whether at home, in the colonies, or in *foreign rival states :* and viewing colonies as foreign states, in so far as commercial intercourse is concerned.

So far has this anti-colonial spirit and theoretical habit prevailed, that although a reciprocity clause appeared on the margin of the new Navigation Bill, the Government rejected the clauses requisite to implement reciprocity. *The Economist, The Morning Chronicle, Manchester Guardian,* &c., ridicule the idea of reciprocity, and contend for abolition of all differential duties and preferences to colonies.

A glance at the " principles " of this Association, its reports and other papers, will convince you that our opinions are widely different—we contend for recognition of colonies as integral portions of the empire, and declare that " whatever relations do or may exist with foreigners, we consider free, unrestricted trade with the colonies to be indispensable."

The argument is detailed in *The Daily Mail* of the 23rd, in a critique on *The Economist*, which last paper seems preparing to modify its principles on colonial connection, thereby indicating a modification of ministerial opinions.

I have the honour to be, Sir,

Your most obedient servant,

G. SUTHERLAND, *Secretary.*

The Hon. George Moffat, M. L. C., Montreal.

(Copy.)

COMMITTEE ROOMS, 12, S. Hanover Street,
Glasgow, 31st Aug., 1849.

SIR,—I beg to hand you the address of the Glasgow Reciprocity Association. A duplicate has been sent to Earl Grey.

It is in contemplation to render this address a more public expression, by adapting it for general signature; in order to do so, certain preliminaries are requisite, which the working committee of the Association have not had time to complete. Rather than delay the enclosed document, it is now sent, officially signed by the chairman and secretary.

I have the honour to be, Sir,

Your most obedient servant,

GEORGE SUTHERLAND.

The Hon. George Moffat, M. L. C., &c.

(Copy.)

To the Members of the British American League, the various Constitutional Societies, and branches thereof, and to the friends of British Connection generally in Canada and the other British North American provinces; the Address of the Glasgow Reciprocity and Industrial Asociatsion.

The undersigned, believing the objects of the above-named societies to be " the promotion of constitutional principles, and the maintenance of British connection," as set forth in the *Toronto Colonist* of 1st June, and more fully in the address of the " British Constitutional Society of the Home District," in same paper of 5th June, beg to call attention to the accompanying "Principles and Objects" of this Association. These are

"To obtain Free Trade with Foreign States, on the basis of a true and equitable reciprocity, and to adopt all reasonable and legitimate means to promote the interests of British and Colonial industry."

The objects thus indicated are fully explained in the Report of the first public meeting of the Association, held in the Merchant's Hall of this city, on the 18th of May.

Believing our countrymen in the colonies to be desirous of remaining connected with the parent state, we solicit their co-operation and sympathy in the great work of preserving the unity and prosperity of the empire.

Our sentiments are indicated by quotations such as these :—" That a one-sided system must result in the decay of our home, colonial and foreign trade ;" that "loss of employment has arisen from the decline of our colonial trade ;" that "it was the duty of the British Legislature to have established free trade with the colonies to the utmost extent warranted by the state of the revenue ;" that "free trade ought to have been begun and completed in our home and colonial trades, before proceeding to give to our foreign rivals the unrestricted, untaxed, unreciprocated privilege of competing in British markets with heavily-taxed British industry ;" that "free trade with our own colonies would contribute largely to increase and consolidate the industrial, commercial, and political relations of Great Britain, not only with the said colonies, but also with foreign powers ;" and "that the interests of this empire require complete freedom of trade with all its colonies and dependencies."

Our objects, as regard the colonies, are :—

"To obtain free trade with the British colonies, recognizing them as integral portions of the empire, by treating coasting and colonial trade on similar principles.

"To procure and circulate authentic information regarding native and colonial industry and interests, to watch the character of all measures introduced into the Imperial and Colonial Legislatures which affect our industrial interests, and to promote and maintain a harmonious intercourse between all sections of the British empire." In short, our countrymen cannot fail to perceive that, whatever relations do or may exist with foreigners, *we consider free, unrestricted trade with the colonies to be indispensable.*

We beg to call attention to those high or prohibitory duties levied in Canada upon British goods—duties which have not benefitted the colonial revenue, and have tended to alienate the colonists and the home producers from each other. This subject was explained in a memorial sent last year to the Colonial Office, from Glasgow, of which a copy is enclosed.

There are many considerations which ought to induce the British, both at home and in the colonies, to preserve that connection, by which a generous and powerful nation is enabled to recognise, assist and protect her people in every clime, and to combine under one flag, millions who glory in the name of Englishmen.

There is every reason—moral, political and economical—for strengthening and reforming the colonial connection.

The British Constitution admits, not in words merely, but in acts and institutions, "That all men are born free" that "Every man's house is his castle"— that "The moment a slave sets foot on British ground, his chains fall from him."

These maxims and safeguards of liberty and justice might require to be compromised or surrendered in the event of annexation to the American Union.

The security of property in land in British America is at present ascertained and guaranteed in a manner it could not possibly be in the event of a foreign legislature assuming the sovereignty of the colonial crown lands, and properties held of the crown.

An influx of settlers from the States, taking possession of territory in virtue of land-scrip, or other powers issued at Washington, might unsettle many existing tenures, landmarks and local boundaries.

B

The existing system of taxation in British America, with its comparatively moderate import duties, are more favourable to the development of her resources, and more consonant to the habits of the colonists, than the high duties and direct taxation system of the States of the Union.

Under the guarantees and encouragements of the British Government, English capital flows into Canada, and would flow still more freely if the usury laws, the bankrupt and tenure laws, were amended, as they would be even under the dominion of the United States. England has mainly contributed to the improvement of those magnificent water communications which, when completed, will enable Canada to compete with those of the Union.

The colonists of the Northern provinces ought not to forget that the vast resources of immense unopened territory—the fisheries, the numerous and excellent harbours, the forests, the cleared land, the minerals—are all, by every law of nature and of nations, British; and that to the North American colonists, aided by England, belong, by the way of the St. Lawrence and Lakes, the trade of the far West, a trade only yet in its infancy, and capable of such extension as defies calculation. The colonists ought to consider well the advantages they possess, to sympathise and co-operate with their countrymen at home in obtaining reforms and just concessions from the Imperial Legislature, rather than countenance any party who, to serve private ends, may suggest separation from the protection, and wealth, and power of Britain, in order to begin a competition with the rival states of the Union.

The " Glasgow Reciprocity Association " solicits the co-operation, of colonists in procuring commercial reforms, domestic and colonial, in counteracting ignorance, and interested prejudice in this country, so that this and similar associations may be enable to anticipate the increasing attention and favour with which the British public are evidently disposed to view the just claims of the colonists.

If the misconceptions, and ignorance, and obstinacy of men in power have been injurious to the colonies, how much more detrimental must these have been to the Empire!

Let the British at home and in the colonies combine their efforts to overcome the neglect, the ignorance and mistakes of which so many complain, assured that these grievances cannot long be permitted to remain, by a nation ever desirous of promoting the honour and the happiness of its members, both at home and in the most distant regions.

Glasgow, 30th August, 1849.

HUGH TENNENT, *Convener.*
GEORGE SUTHERLAND, *Secretary.*

(Copy of Memorial.)

To the Right Hon. Earl Grey, Secretary of State for the Colonies, the Memorial of the undersigned merchants, manufacturers, shipowners and other inhabitants of Glasgow,

Humbly sheweth—That your memorialists are interested in the manufacturing prosperity of the United Kingdom, and in the export of commodities to the colonies.

That the Provincial Government of Canada, in their last session, passed an act, viz. :—" The 10 and 11 Victoria, chap. 31 and 32, for repealing and consolidating the present duties of customs in the province of Canada, and for other purposes therein mentioned, to take effect on 5th January, 1848," but now awaiting the Royal sanction.

Your memorialsts observe with regret and alarm the formidable augmentation of Import Duties on British products and manufactures, proposed by that Act, as specified in the " Table of Custom Duties," published by her Majesty's printers in Canada.

That while the mother-country admits the staple products of Canada, either duty free, or at discriminating duties, that colony proposes to levy duties on British manufactures, varying from five to thirty per *centum ad valorem;* and that the average rate of said duties is equivalent to 12¾ per cent., the complex character and numerous different rates in the "table," rendering an exact estimate unattainable.

That the other great colonies in the East and West Indies and Australia, have hitherto imposed low duties, averaging about three and a half per cent.

That the act, complained of proposes to place the mother country in a more unfavourable position than the very colonies under her dominion, namely, the "other British North American colonies," the native produce and manufactures of which are proposed to be admitted into Canada free of duty, provided the said colonies shall receive Canadian produce and manufactures on the same terms.

That the said colonial act proposes to place the mother country in a more unfavourable position than the United States of America, in so far as it repeals the differential duties hitherto maintained in favour of British manufactures.

We shall deem it a hardship if, as British subjects, paying taxes, of which a portion is expended in the government and defence of that colony, our goods shall be admitted on less favourable terms than those of the United States manufacturer, who contributes nothing to that expense, and who may thus, by unfair competition, be enabled ultimately to drive the British merchant and manufacturer out of that colonial market.

For these reasons, as well as for the maintenance of the "British connection" in America, your memorialists pray that when said act shall come under your Lordship's consideration, it may not receive the consent of the Crown.

Mr. Dixon asked and obtained permission to lay on the table a copy of a Resolution, as follows :—

" That whereas, after mature deliberation and discussion, this Convention has recorded its solemn conviction, that the social, commercial and political condition of the British North American Provinces, and more especially the Province of Canada is such, that a much longer continuance in their present state will lead to confusion and civil strife, and that the remedies best calculated to restore prosperity to their drooping interests are, a Union of the British North American Provinces, Protection to Native Industry, and a rigid Economy in the administration of their several Governments ; and that in order to secure these great blessings with the least possible delay, it is highly necessary to call the attention of the people of Canada to the principles upon which it would be beneficial and safe to unite and consolidate the several interests of the said Provinces.'

" It is therefore Resolved—That the principles best adapted for securing these objects are—

" First—The full enjoyment and exercise, by each Province, of all the social, religious and political freedom guaranteed to us by our present institutions, or as they may hereafter be amended, to promote our social comfort and happiness, by affording us the perfect control of all that is strictly local in our government, including our roads and canals (with the exception of the great thoroughfares open to the United Provinces,) together with our civil jurisprudence and industrial pursuits.

" Second—By establishing a perfect equality in inter-Provincial rights—in the participation of equal trading and commercial privileges—the free and full use (upon terms of strict equality) of rivers, canals and roads, together with an equal distribution of the public burthen and public revenue, in proportion to the consumption of each Province.

" Third—By a perfect and untrammeled intercourse with each Province in carrying out the principle of free trade amongst ourselves as a united people.

" Fourth—By consolidating our interests and wants in one general principle of legislation for the assistance, direction and control of our commerce, in such a way as to impress it with a national character, and preserve our industrial pursuits from a ruinous competition, and an unequal pressure upon each other—by creating and sustaining a national credit and self-respect throughout the world,—by establishing one general code of criminal jurisprudence, a general and uniform currency, and a general bankrupt law,—by well regulated postal communications, and by a willingness to yield minor advantages for the general good."

Mr. Strachan asked and obtained permission to lay on the table a copy of a sketch of a Constitution for British North America, as follows :—

" *Sketch of a Constitution for British North America, humbly submitted to this Convention by John Strachan, delegate from Huron.*

" 1st. That the Canadas, with New Brunswick, Nova Scotia, Prince Edward's Island, and Newfoundland, be joined in one Federal Union under the name of " British North America."

" 2nd. The Queen's title to be then, Queen of the United Kingdom of Great Britain, Ireland and British North America—British North America to have a Secretary and office in Downing Street to itself, and to be governed by a Viceroy with a Federal Legislature.

3rd. Each Province to have a separate Government for the management of local matters ; the Legislative Council of each Province to be elective, by a Special Election, with a higher qualification, both on the part of the Electors and Elected, than is required in the Provincial Assembly.

" 4th. The Legislative powers to be granted to the Federal Government, shall be vested in a General Assembly or Parliament, consisting of the Governor-General or Viceroy, a Legislative Council and House of Assembly. Such General Assembly or Parliament, to continue six years from the day of returning the writs for choosing the same, and no longer, subject, nevertheless, to be sooner prorogued or dissolved, by the Governor-General or Viceroy.

" 5th. The Legislative Council shall be composed of six members from each Province, to be chosen by the Governor, Lieutenant-Governor, or person administering the government of the several Colonies, from the respective Legislative Councils, or of persons selected by the Crown from the most prominent men in the respective Provinces, or of persons elected by the Legislatures themselves, from among their own number ; the period of their service to be six years, one third to retire every second year.

" 6th. The House of Assembly shall be composed of ——— members, chosen by the Provincial Assemblies from among their own number, or by a special election, but with a higher qualification, both on the part of the electors and elected, than is required in the Provincial Assemblies.

" 7th. That a deputation of three members from the Legislative Council, selected by the Governor-General from that body, or three out of six proposed by the Legislative Council for his choice, and six chosen by the House of Assembly from among its own members, have seats in the House of Commons.

" 8th. This General Legislature or Parliament shall have power—

' 1st. To lay on and collect taxes, duties and imports—the same to be uniform throughout the Union.

' 2nd. To assume and pay the debts of the several Provinces, and provide for the peace and welfare of the Union.

' 3rd. To establish uniform Commercial Regulations between the different Provinces, and between them and Foreign Countries, provided the same be not repugnant to the Laws of the United Kingdom.

' 4th. To determine all disputes that may arise between the Provinces.

' 5th. To regulate the Navigation of Rivers and Lakes, common to two or more Provinces, or common to any Province or Provinces, and a Foreign Power.

' 6th. To open internal communication for the general advantage, such as roads, canals, railroads, steam navigation, &c.

' 7th. To establish and regulate the Post Office and Post Roads, within the Union.

' 8th. To adopt and establish an uniform system of Militia Laws; and to provide for calling forth the Militia—to execute the laws, to suppress insurrection and repel invasion.'

" 9th. All bills for raising revenue, shall originate in the House of Assembly, but the Legislative Council may propose or concur with amendments, as in other bills.

"10th. There shall be a Supreme Court to take cognizance of causes respecting the breach of the Union laws, and questions between inhabitants of the different Provinces, and between them and foreigners.

"11th. This tribunal shall likewise be a Court of Appeal in certain cases from the Provincial Courts, and its decision shall be final. All proceedings to be in the English language, not only in the Supreme Court, but in all the inferior Courts of the Colonies.

"12th. Persons charged in any Province with treason, felony, or other crime, who shall flee from justice, and be found in any of the other Provinces of the Union, shall, on demand of the Executive authority of the Colony from which they fled, be delivered up to be removed into the Province having jurisdiction of the crime.

"13th. The portion of the Revenue at the disposal of the general Legislature for public purposes, shall be the surplus after defraying the expenses of the Civil Government of the respective Provinces, which shall be settled by general enactment.

"14th. Several other powers, such as impeachment, regulation, and protection of the fisheries, &c. &c. &c., might be conferred on the supreme Legislature.
     (Signed)   " JOHN STRACHAN,
                     " Senior Delegate,
" In Convention,   County of Huron,
" Toronto, Nov. 5, 1849.' "

Mr. MILLER moved, seconded by Mr. R. McDONALD,

That it be resolved, That it is a matter of regret to this convention, that the subject of a separation of this Colony from the Mother Country, and of Annexation to the United States of America, has been openly advocated by a portion of the press and inhabitants of this Province; and this Convention unhesitatingly records its entire disapprobation of this course, and calls upon all well-wishers of their country to discountenance it by every means in their power.

Mr. HAMILTON moved in amendment, seconded by Mr. G. DUGGAN, that the resolution be not adopted, but that the following be substituted:—

That it is wholly inexpedient to discuss the question of Annexation at this Convention, the loyalty of whose members cannot be questioned, and amongst whom, as a body, there is found no individual to advocate any such obnoxious principle.—Which was lost.

The main motion was then put and carried unanimously.

Mr. R. R. SMILLIE introduced a motion respecting postal arrangements.—Which was put from the chair, and lost.

Mr. VANKOUGHNET moved, seconded by Mr. DEEDES,

That it be resolved, That in accordance with the suggestion contained in the report of the Committee of Conference on the union, already adopted; and inasmuch as time does not admit of this Convention, in its present session, digesting the principles of a constitution for the union; a deputation of gentlemen be selected by the Central Society, who shall be requested to meet, in the city of Halifax, in Nova Scotia, at some early and convenient day, to be fixed by themselves, such gentlemen as may then and there assemble from the other provinces, to discuss the terms of the union; and that all papers submitted to this Convention, in reference to such union, as containing any suggestions in regard to a constitution, he submitted to the gentlemen who may so assemble at Halifax, for their consideration, and with the view that, using the same and all other possible means for obtaining information, they may prepare a report—to be submitted to the Central Society, and to this or any future convention of the League, as also to the public—containing such information and suggestions as may be thought useful.—Which was carried.

Mr. J. DUGGAN moved, seconded by Mr. DARBY,

That Messrs. Samuel Thompson, Francis Neale, John W. Gamble and Hugh Scobie, be a committee to superintend the printing of the proceedings of this session of the convention.—Which was carried.

The Convention then adjourned until to-morrow at 9 o'clock, a. m.

WEDNESDAY, NOV. 7, 1849.

The Convention met, pursuant to adjournment.

Mr. GAMBLE brought up the following report :—

The Committee appointed to enquire and report what amendments to the constitution of the League, and appointments to the Central Committee, become necessary in consequence of the removal of the seat of Government from Montreal, beg to report that it will be necessary to increase the number of the Executive Committee to twenty, for which purpose the 8th clause of the Constitution should be amended, by striking out the word "ten" and inserting "twenty," and by adding the words "be it always nevertheless understood and declared, that any officer or officers of the League may be appointed or removed, and the places of any resignations supplied, at any meeting of the Convention." They further report that the following officers have resigned :—The Hon. George Moffatt, the Hon. William Allan, the Hon. William Morris, David Gorrie, William Gordon Mack, J. Helder Isaacson and H. E. Montgomery, Esquires; and your Committee further report, that it is not only their wish, but they believe the unanimous desire of the Convention, that the Hon. George Moffatt should remain as President of the League, and that he be respectfully requested to withdraw his resignation. All of which is respectfully submitted.

J. W. GAMBLE.
EDWARD G. O'BRIEN.
W. GORDON MACK.

Toronto, 7th Nov. 1849.   SAM. ROWLANDS.

Mr. O'BRIEN moved, seconded by Mr. DEEDES,

That it be resolved, That the report now submitted by the Committee on the Constitution of the League, be adopted.—Which was carried.

Mr. O'BRIEN moved, seconded by Mr. PARKE,

That it be resolved, That the additional number of members to the Central Committee, together with the vacancies reported, shall be now filled up by the Convention.—Which was carried.

Mr. O'BRIEN moved, seconded by Mr. LANGTON,

That it be resolved, That on the re-assembling of the Convention, all members be required to produce a certificate, signed by the President, and countersigned by the Secretary, of the Branch for which such member is elected.—Which was carried.

Mr. GAMBLE moved, seconded by Mr. MAIR,

That it be resolved, That a committee be appointed to nominate proper persons to fill the vacancies in the central committee, and that the same do consist of Messrs. Vankoughnet, W. S. McDonald, and Read.—Which was carried.

Mr. HAMILTON moved, seconded by Mr. AIKMAN,

That it be resolved, That the constitution of the League shall be altered, by making provision for the representation to which the several branch leagues shall be entitled in convention, on the following scale, viz. :

For each branch league of one hundred members, one representative.

For each branch of three hundred members, two representatives.

For each branch of six hundred members, three representatives.

For each branch of one thousand, four representatives; and for every additional thousand members, one representative.—Which was lost.

Mr. MACK moved, seconded by Mr. A. J. McDONELL,

That it be resolved, That the continued presence of Lord Elgin, as Governor General of Canada, is injurious to the interests of the people of this province, and calculated to undermine the loyalty of her Majesty's subjects.—Which was carried unanimously.

Mr. W. S. MACDONALD brought up the following report :

The committee appointed to recommend officers, in lieu of those resigned, beg to report that they recommend to this convention to appoint J. W. Gamble as a Vice President, in place of Hon. W. Allan,—George Benjamin, Esq., as Vice President, in place of Hon. W. Morris—and, in lieu of the members of the Executive Committee resigned, Hugh Scobie, Esq., of Toronto, George Rykert, Esq., of St. Catherines, Stuart McKechnie, Esq., of Cobourg, Capt. Boyd, of Yonge Street, Benjamin Switzer, Esq., of Streetsville ; and, to complete the additional number required by the amended constitution, Dr. Hamilton, of Dundas, Thomas Brunskill, Esq., of Toronto, George P. Ridout, Esq., of Toronto, Lewis Moffatt, Esq., of Toronto, J. G. Bowes, Esq., of Toronto, A. C. Hamilton, Esq., of St. Catherines, John O. Hatt, Esq., of Hamilton, F. Neale, Esq., of Yonge Street, James Brown, Esq., of Toronto, P. M. Vankoughnet, Esq., of Toronto ; Corresponding Secretary, S. Thompson, Esq., of

Toronto; Recording Secretary, R. Cooper, Esq., of Toronto; Treasurer, John Duggan, Esq., of Toronto.

W. S. MACDONALD, *Chairman.*

7th November, 1849.

Which was adopted.

Mr. FERRES moved, seconded by Mr. NEALE,

That it be resolved, That the thanks of the Convention are due to Messrs. W. G. Mack, as Corresponding Secretary; John Helder Isaacson, as Secretary; and H. E. Montgomerie, as Treasurer; for their past services in their respective capacities.—Which was carried unanimously.

Mr. MACK returned thanks for himself and his late colleagues.

The Chairman having left the chair, and Mr. J. W. Gamble having taken it,

Mr. O'BRIEN moved, seconded by Mr. STRACHAN,

That it be resolved, That the thanks of this Convention are due, and are hereby tendered to the Honourable George Moffatt, President of this Convention, for his urbanity and dignified deportment in the chair while presiding over this convention during its present session.—Which was carried unanimously.

The Honourable GEORGE MOFFATT returned thanks.

Mr. MACKECHNIE moved, seconded by Mr. J. YOUNG,

That it be resolved, That the Chairman be requested to convey the thanks of this Convention to the Mayor and Corporation of Toronto, for their kindness in granting it the use of the City Hall during its present session.—Which was carried.

Mr. LANGTON moved, seconded by Mr. J. W. GAMBLE,

That it be resolved, That whereas a difference has arisen in this Convention upon the question of elective institutions, and whereas the majority of the members present have declared that the legislative council should continue to be appointed by the Crown, subject to limitation as to number, and not be elected by the people as contended for by the minority, and this Convention having disposed of the other business brought before it: Be it therefore resolved, That this convention be now adjourned to a day to be hereafter named by the Central Committee, with a view to the several branches of the British American League pronouncing their opinion, and instructing their delegates upon the question of the concession of elective institutions to Canada, as an appendage to the British Crown; and that the several branches do make a return to the Secretary of the Central Society, Toronto, of the delegates whom they may appoint, on or before the first day of January next.—Which was carried unanimously.

And the Convention adjourned accordingly.

APPENDIX.

REPORT OF DEBATES

AT THE

CONVENTION OF DELEGATES OF THE BRITISH AMERICAN LEAGUE,

*Held at Toronto, C. W., on Thursday, Nov. 1, and by Adjournment
on the 2nd, 3rd, 5th, 6th and 7th of November, 1849.*

FRIDAY, Nov. 2d, 10 o'clock, A. M.

Mr. J. W. GAMBLE moved the first of the resolutions of which he had given notice.

Resolved—That the condition of this province calls loudly upon all lovers of peace and good government, speedily to adopt measures whereby the present excitement may be allayed, public tranquillity restored, and existing political differences merged in one paramount sentiment—the good of our common country. Since the burning of the parliament houses, disturbance has followed disturbance, and riot has succeeded riot in quick succession; on several occasions human blood has been shed—the law violated with impunity; while the government, by their ineffectual attempts to repress these disorders, have been brought into contempt. Exciting and irritating political questions, involving the dismemberment of this colony from the empire, are openly advocated, engendering discontent, discord and fierce political animosities; rancorous feelings are separating neighbour from neighbour, to the hindrance and neglect of business, the interruption of industry, the loss of confidence, and the destruction of credit; the public mind is becoming vitiated by these excesses, a spirit of insubordination to the laws is manifested, which, if allowed to prevail, threatens to burst asunder the bonds of society, and lead to the most deplorable consequences—anarchy, confusion and civil strife.

He said, he believed the resolution did not contain one single word but what every gentleman present in the Convention was prepared to respond to, with regard to the condition of the country. But at the outset, before entering into those matters, he would state the plan on which he proposed the discussion should be conducted; the first resolution contained the foundation on which he hoped hereafter to raise some superstructure, the object was to state the exact condition of the country, that was a mere question of fact; do things exist as stated in that resolution? If so, that was the foundation on which they were to build, there could be but little discussion upon that point. Neither did he think there would be much discussion about the second resolution, because he was satisfied that no member of the Convention would gainsay what was there stated of the necessity that the feelings and opinions of the people of this country should be properly represented in the Legislative Assembly. There might be a difference of opinion in regard to the manner of the application necessary, in order to obtain the object in view. Some gentlemen would be in favor of the present Parliament being dissolved and an application made for that purpose, and others would advise an application to be made to the present Assembly. He did not think that the two first resolutions would give rise to much discussion, but upon the third resolution, of which he had given notice, all these great questions now agitating the public mind would be discussed, and amongst them the question of Annexation, and he hoped that those in favour of that measure would be prepared with their strongest arguments and ready to bring them forward, as he did not want to be raising up men of straw to knock them down again.—He should not occupy much of the time of the Convention with any introductory remarks he had to make, but he must say a few words on the first resolution which was to be the foundation on which he hoped to build. Supposing a stranger were to enter this Province at the western extremity and proceed through the various channels of intercourse, occasionally leaving them and going into the interior of the country—crossing it from south to north and back again, and if he pursued his route to Quebec and the far east, he would find that there was one engrossing topic occupying the attention of the whole people of Canada, and that was the political condition of the country. (Hear, hear.)—If he were to travel in steamboats he would find the passengers gathered together into little knots most earnestly discussing the same theme; if he leaves the steamboat and goes to his hotel, what does he find there? just the same sort of thing; the merchants and lawyers leaving their respective business, people engaged in the various branches of industry, are all there talking of annexation, independence and British connection, and of the changes necessary to be accomplished, and if he went into the public streets he would find the same there, and in fact from one end of the Province to the other. (Hear, hear.) He (Mr. Gamble) had had an opportunity of testing it, and he would declare that he never in his life remembered the Province to be in such a state as it is at present; men's minds are excited to the utmost and all are intent upon some change or other. These are the questions in which the people feel that their highest and deepest interests are concerned, and they naturally produce an excitement and difference of opinion which lead to irritation and ill-feeling. The discussion of these questions was leading to the most serious evils in the country. He considered the excitement to be an evil and the irritation and bad passions engendered to be a still greater evil, and more than this, it leads to questions of so deep and mysterious a nature that people sometimes forget the boundaries that they ought not to pass, and sometimes from that which is perfectly right and proper step over the boundary into that which is criminal; this had perhaps been the case with regard to the discussion of the questions of annexation and independence, and not only this but our position is such that hardly anything can occur but some great political event is attached to it. For instance, His Excellency, Lord Elgin, could not move from one end of the Province to the other without riot and confusion following him almost wherever he went, (hear, hear,) and if it had not been for the most strenuous and determined exertions of those very men whose feelings had been outraged (loud cries of hear, hear) his progress from one end of this Province to the other would have been tracked in blood. (Loud cheers.) This showed the state of feeling existing in the country, and he would ask ought such a state of things to continue? Another thing which had greatly tended to increase their excitement and irritation was the question of the removal of the Seat of Government, which had made the people of Montreal almost frantic—(hear hear)—and had produced no small excitement in Toronto also, but as Toronto had proved to be the favoured spot, the oil had in s me measure calmed the troubled waters. (Hear hear.) A feeling of general discontent prevails from one end of the Province to the other. Look at the different classes into which the community is divided.— The productive classes are divided into the producers, the fashioners, and the exchangers. Take the producer first—go to the farmer and ask if he is satisfied? He will tell you no, and why? Because he cannot get a remunerative reward for his labour; he is not satisfied because his neighbour, who is only separated from him by an almost imaginary line, or by a river, gets 25 or 30 per cent. more for his produce than he can get. Go then to the manufacturers and ask them if they are contented—many of the few factories there are in this Province are closed—and the manufacturers will tell you, too, they are not contented; that the Government do not consider their interests;

that their interests are neglected, and consequently they are discontented. Go then to the exchanger—the merchant, and ask him if he is satisfied—if business is plenty—if he can readily get rid of his goods, and get paid for them, is money plenty, has he the means of going a-head, and extending his business? He would tell you he is not satisfied, and that without some great political change he can never prosper. But there was yet another class—the drones; to this class belong the gentlemen of the legal profession, ask those gentlemen if they are satisfied? Oh yes, they are satisfied—suits plenty—costs heavy—fees and profits large, and Judgeships in expectancy; every thing is as it should be, they desire no change, they are satisfied—they are the only satisfied class in the country. (Hear and cheers.) He would like to know what proportion this class, the drones, including the literary gentlemen, bear to the whole population. All these classes, the non-producers, put together, only amount to 20 per cent. of the whole population; all the other classes are dissatisfied. He now turned to that part of the resolution which spoke of the riots and disturbances that had occurred in the country; he did not speak of the causes of these riots, he merely stated the fact, and that the Parliament Houses had been burnt down. He for one was very sorry for that occurrence, and he was sure that every gentleman in the Convention felt so also; but still was it not true, and was he not justified in saying that disturbance had followed disturbance, and riot succeeded riot in quick succession since these things commenced in Montreal? (Hear, hear.) What was seen from one end of the Province to the other? In every little village there was effigy burning at least, and that had been decided by one of the first authorities in the land to be a species of sedition. (Hear hear.) If it had been confined to this kind of thing, although it was seditious, it might have been passed by and forgotten, but there were other things which they could not forget? They could not forget when they found bodies of their fellow subjects arrayed one against another with arms in their hands; when men's animosities and hatred were so excited against each other by politics, that they did not hesitate to take each other's lives; they could not forget that human blood had been shed, and not once or twice, but in numerous instances, from one end of the Province to the other. It was time indeed for all good men to rise up and say, these things shall not be— we will not disgrace ourselves as a social and christian community—we will have no bloodshed here—(cheers)—and if those who are placed in authority to govern the country lack the ability, or the inclination, or the power to put them down, a right and proper remedy must be provided. (Cheers) The last of these disturbances was in Bytown, and he (Mr. Gamble) had been assured by a gentleman of opposite politics to himself who was present, that there were on the second day of the riots some 750 men on each side arrayed against each other with muskets, fowling pieces, and every species of arms; and although no collision took place, it could not have been prevented but for a handful of Her Majesty's troops, who fortunately interposed between the parties. What a horrible thing it would have been had these bodies of our fellow subjects been permitted to come into collision, and spill each other's blood about some political question, which both are interested in having decided in a proper manner. Those at the head of the government have incurred an awful responsibility, and how has it been discharged? Has the law been visited on these transgressors, or has it been violated with impunity? Have any steps been taken to bring the parties guilty of the burning of the Parliament House to punishment? Yes! some steps have been taken, innocent men have been incarcerated on the most flimsy evidence, for the gratification of vindictive party feelings. (Loud cheers.) Had anything been done with regard to the riots and effigy burning throughout the Province? Could any gentleman present point out to them one single instance in which the transgressors of the law had been brought to punishment? With regard to the Bytown riots, which occurred only the other day the evidence of which was fresh on the spot—had these rioters been brought to justice? He was told not; the parties had been held to bail. And all this because the government dare not take any steps; the ground on which they stand is too ticklish. Those who sought to reward past treason cannot consistently punish sedition. (Cheers.) He then came to another act which he for one deeply regretted. Much as he regretted the burning of the Parliament House, he regretted the Montreal Manifesto more. (Hear, hear.) True, it was couched in specious language, but it was to the spirit they must look. Then, too, certain resolutions were published in a paper there offering *a reward for the very best work on Annexation.* (Hear, hear.) Perhaps he might be wrong in his idea of the law, but he imagined that a few years ago it would have been a dangerous thing for any person to put forth such an advertisement, (hear, hear), or for any newspaper editor to publish it. He was sorry for the Montreal manifesto; it was a most unwise, injudicious step, even if the parties themselves wished to accomplish annexation. Was the spirit in which it was written strictly in accordance with the laws of the country? These things together were producing a most discontented and embittered feeling throughout the country, which it was melancholy to contemplate. The next thing were the interference of all this with the business of the country. Instead of each one attending to his own business, and forwarding the true interests of the country, his mind is filled with politics, and the business of the country is interrupted. Nor is individual credit alone affected by these fierce political discussions, but the public credit is likewise damaged. (Hear, hear.) He (Mr. Gamble) had been told, upon good

authority, that certain moneys which were necessary could not be obtained, because the state of the country was such that no man having money to invest would lend it here. (Hear, hear.) What would be the consequence of this continual infringement of the law without the transgressors being punished? Do not people even now do, without hesitation, what but a short time ago they would have trembled to have done? Are not their minds so vitiated that they do not hesitate to perpetrate acts of violence, and to infringe the law? If these things were facts, let the Convention say so by adopting this resolution. What would be the end of this state of things, unless prompt and effectual means were taken to check its progress? He (Mr. Gamble) was of opinion that it would not stop short of a civil war. Gentlemen might say what they pleased, and think what they pleased, but they were at that moment standing on a volcano, and some small and trivial circumstance might ignite the combustibles, and in a moment blow this province into confusion. He hoped that such a thing might never occur, but that the Convention would have the firmness to act on what they knew was coming, and to endeavour to avoid consequences so deplorable, and which they would all lament to the last day of their existence (Cheers.) He begged to move the first resolution.

Mr. T. McKinnon, (Bytown,) seconded the motion and bore testimony to the truth of Mr. Gamble's remarks about the late disturbances in Bytown.

Mr. Aikman thought that part of the resolution which alluded to the burning of the Parliament House unnecessary, and he had therefore prepared an amendment to strike it out. That matter had been taken up at the Kingston meeting, and he thought that if they wished to quiet the public mind, they should avoide any further allusion to those exciting topics.

Mr. A. J. McDonell seconded the amendment on the ground that he wished nothing to appear on the resolutions of the Convention, that might in the slightest degree appear to imply satisfaction in Lord Elgin's course. If Mr. Gamble would consent to add one line to his resolution, giving the cause of the riots, he (Mr. McD.) would support it, but unless he would do that, he must adhere to the amendment. By passing the resolution in its present shape, the Convention would indirectly censure the people of Montreal by saying that they have thrown the province into confusion, when in fact Lord Elgin and the Rebellion Losses Bill, and not the people of Montreal, have done it. (Cheers.) He agreed fully with Mr. Gamble's resolution, he thought it contained nothing but the truth, but in its present form it was capable of being distorted, and to prevent any misconception, he would rather that the causes which have led to these riots should be stated decidedly and manfully.

Mr. Rolland McDonald agreed in a great deal that had fallen from the mover and seconder of the amendment; he thought it would be wrong to allow the resolution to go to the country as it stood. If they referred to the burning of the parliament house, and the riots in Montreal that had resulted from it, they ought to go still further back, and state the causes, or *the* moving cause, that brought about all these things; but he thought that if they would strike out three or four words, and substitute three or four others in their place, that the resolution would do very well. He would strike out "burning of the parliament house," and put in instead " passing of the Rebellion-losses bill." There was another thing which struck him, with regard to Mr. Gamble's second resolution: the first resolution proposed nothing; it merely established the groundwork to go upon, but if the first resolution were a correct statement of the condition of the country, as he believed it was, would it be safe to hold a general election? He did not desire to speak decidedly on that point, but he wished that they should approach the question cautiously. If it be true that the country is bordering on a civil war, is that the time to have a general election—will it tranquilize the public mind? He believed that if there was a general election at this moment, there would not be an election from one end of the Province to the other, where there would not be bloodshed. (Hear, hear.) Even in the Niagara District, one of the most peaceably disposed districts in the province, an election could not take place without riot and bloodshed. Was this the time for a lover of his country and of his kind to ask the Governor-General to dissolve Parliament? He should say not: (hear, hear,) and he should say further, that it was better for the Convention not to enter into matters that would have a tendency to keep up bitter feelings. Then, there were, he knew, many gentlemen in the Assembly, who would never consent to address the present Governor-General for any thing, and the present House of Assembly could not be dissolved without asking him to do it. There were many who felt that the country could never be at peace whilst his feet tread upon our soil.— (Great cheering.) Such was his (Mr. McDonald's opinion, and he had expressed it at the last Convention, when he voted that it was essential for the well being of the Province, that that individual should go home; but it was unnecessary to say anything more on that subject now, and he desired by everything he might say in the Convention, not to increase the excitement, but the contrary. (Hear, hear.) He would further remark; *en passant*, that when Mr. Gamble stated that the legal profession was perfectly satisfied with the state of the country, he was not giving himself the full benefit of his argument— the lawyers were not contented. He wished it to be understood that the profession to which he had the honour to belong, never could prosper amongst a poor people. (Hear, hear.) Poor people cannot afford to go to law, and people won't go to law with poor people, Mr. Gamble stated that there was a great deal of suing going on, and that the lawyers were filling their pockets; but that was not the case; people were actually afraid to sue, for fear of having to pay the costs; the lawyers were never so prosperous as

when the country was prosperous, for the people could then afford to go to law with their neighbours upon the slightest dispute. He concluded by stating his intention to move an amendment that the words, " burning of the Parliament House," be struck out, and the words, " passing of the Rebellion Losses Bill," be substituted.

Mr. GEORGE CRAWFORD (Brockville,) prefectly agreed with the former part of the resolution, but there was one clause which he could not agree with, and that was the clause which referred to the Annexation movement now going on in Montreal, and which stated that the discussion of the question of Annexation gave rise to " fierce political animosities." He denied that the document sent forth to the world, by the annexationists of Montreal, had caused these political animosities. There never was a document emanating from any body of men more temperate or couched in more moderate language than that document, and he doubted if any document involving questions of such magnitude had been discussed so calmly and quietly. He had seen some of the irritation, which formerly existed between the radicals and tories; that was where the excitement existed, and not between the annexationists and anti-annexationists. (Hear, hear.) He was for letting the discussion of Annexation go on, so as to prepare the public mind for it when it does come. Every man in the colony to whom he had spoken admitted that a time must come when we shall be separated from England; and if so, he thought it high time we were beginning to discuss the matter. The riot and disturbances which attended Lord Elgin's progress through the country, were not caused by the discussion of Annexation; the insults proceeded from the old loyalist party, and what could be expected from an insulted community, but irritation and violence. He intended, when the proper time came, to move to strike out all the words in the resolution after " the good of our common country "

Mr. HAMILTON (Grantham,) could not see the use of the first resolution, as it merely contained a statement of facts, of which every body was aware. He, for one, should trace the present disorganization of the country. not to the Rebellion Losses Bill, but to the union of the Provinces of Upper and Lower Canada, which led, in fact, to the passing of the objectionable bill; and he might go further back still.

Mr. D. B. READ hoped Mr. Gamble would consent to alter his resolution, so as to meet the views of Mr Rolland McDonald, otherwise he (Mr. R.) would support the amendment

Mr. MacDONALD (Gananoque,) objected to the censure on the signers of the Montreal manifesto, contained in the resolution; he thought that so far from that manifesto having a tendency to promote discontent, discord, and fierce political animosities, it would tend to allay the existing excitement, and that ultimately the country would find out, that the course it recommends is the true remedy for the evils under which we labour. (Cheers.)

Mr. MILLER supported Mr. R. McDonald's amendment.

MR. GEORGE DUGGAN would prefer Mr. McDonald's amendment to the original resolution ; he thought that the circumstances of the country, and the various causes that have led to the prevailing discontent, and the evils that press upon us, were well understood throughout the country, and that it was unnecessary for the Convention to set them forth in a manifesto. He liked Mr. Gowan's resolution, because it came boldly, and broadly, and honestly to the fact, that the country cannot remain in its present state; that was an opinion which he believed was concurred in by three-fourths of the Colony ; he wished to have it broadly stated, and that they should agree to some means by which such a state of things could be brought about, as would enable this colony to continue in a state of harmony and good feeling, and in connection with the parent state if possible. He was prepared to support Mr. Gowan's resolution, and to have it go forth to the country as the deliberate opinion of the delegates.

MR. GAMBLE said that the alterations proposed would completely alter the character of his resolution ; he begged for one to be distinctly understood that he had not come to the Convention for any party purposes, but to devise measures for the good of the country, without respect to party ; and he trusted there was good sense and independence enough in the Convention to stand up for such measures as they conceived to be for the good of their country. The purposed alteration would stamp the character of the resolution, and give it a meaning which it does not now bear. The resolution did not pretend to assign causes for the condition of the country, but simply to assert that such a state of things does exist ; with regard to the first amendment, to leave out the allusion to the burning of the Parliament House, he would ask why should it be left out ? Had not these things taken place ? Was there anything but the truth in the resolution ? He would not insult the members of the Convention by supposing that anything in the resolution could reflect on any one of them, for he was sure that no gentleman present had any thing to do with these matters. (Hear, hear.) Let it not be supposed that, because he alluded to these matters, he did not sympathise with the people who acted imprudently in a moment of ungovernable fury. (Hear, hear.) He did sympathise with them, and he could go further, and state the causes of these occurrences, but he did not attempt to do it in this resolution ; it was intended simply to lay the foundation on which they were to build, and he called upon those gentlemen who had the prosperity of their country at heart to stand by him and carry the resolution. The substitution of the words " Indemnity Bill" would give the resolution a party character, and if that were done he would abandon it and leave other gentlemen to take it up. He denied that the Indemnity Bill was the cause of these occurrences, the depression of trade, and the unfortunate state of the country was the cause, and the Indemnity Bill was the spark that

blew the thing up. With regard to what was said by Mr. Crawford, he had given his (Mr. Gamble's) words a meaning which he never intended them to bear ; was any thing said in the Resolution about the Montreal manifesto ; did that gentleman feel his withers wrung by the allusion to the matter ; was not the annexation question discussed before ever the manifesto appeared ? (A Delegate,—no, it was not.) Was not annexation discussed from one end of the Province to the other before ever the Montreal manifesto appeared ? Could gentlemen deny that ? He did hope there was independence and good sense enough in the Convention to adopt the resolution without altering its character.

Mr. CRAWFORD said, that when the Convention was first forming, it was understood by every one who joined it that all party and irritating subjects should be kept away, but was the course they were now pursuing carrying out that intention ? It was intended, and expected, that a great number of the Reformers of the country would join in the Convention, as it was for the general good of the country ; but he believed no one Reformer had yet joined them, nor would they so long as these irritating subjects were introduced. Let them do away with all those old party distinctions, and endeavour to bring forward such measures as would have a tendency to promote the objects for which the League was originally founded. The bad government was not confined to the present administration ; the party last in power were, in his opinion, just about as bad, and if he thought that the Convention, or the resolutions it might pass, would have a tendency to bring back the late ministry to power, he, for his part, would have nothing whatever to do with it. (Cheers) The object of the Convention was to do away with all party movements, and to get all to join for the general good of the country. He objected to the allusion to the annexation movement in the resolution before the house ; the language made use of was very disrespectful towards the gentlemen in Montreal from whom the manifesto emanated ; it would have a tendency to irritate their minds, and cause several gentlemen belonging to the Convention to withdraw. The amendment he intended to move would do away with these irritating subjects altogether.

Mr. HAMILTON thought the resolution should be somewhat modified ; at present it contained not one word with regard to the commercial state of the country, it simply alluded to the fact of greatly excited political feelings. Mr. Gowan's first resolution was to his mind preferable, because it alluded to the commercial, as well as to the political condition of the Province. He objected to the allusion to the discussion of annexation, because it seemed to cast a direct and positive censure on all who looked to annexation even as a dernier resort ; and he did not think it would have the effect of in any way allaying the existing political excitement.

Mr. DIXON thought it would have been better if the phrase " the burning of the Parliament House" had been left out, as he could see no good likely to arise from reflections on what was past. He would testify to the truth of the resolution, as far as his own quarter was concerned, there was a great deal of rancorous feeling that was loosening the bands of society. The discussion of annexation had a great deal to do with this feeling, and it was natural it should be the case amongst those who entertained a warm attachment to the institutions of the country.

Mr. Aikman's amendment was then put and lost, by a very large majority.

Mr. ROLLAND McDONALD moved to strike out the words "burning of the Parliament House," and substitute "passing of the Rebellion Losses Bill."

Mr. STRACHAN, (Goderich), seconded the amendment. He considered that the allusion to the Rebellion Losses Bill would be no more a party matter than the allusion to the burning of the Parliament House. He bore testimony to the excitement and ill feeling which the discussion of annexation was creating in the western country. He hoped the Convention would take the question up, and at once knock it on the head.

Mr. GOWAN suggested that the words "for some time past" should be substituted for the words "since the burning of the Parliament House." He thought that would meet the views of both sides of the house. (Cries of No, no, and State the truth.) Well, was not that the truth?

Mr. STRACHAN—No, it does not give the cause.

Mr. GOWAN denied that the Rebellion Bill was the whole cause, the causes were in existence long before the passing of that bill. He should vote against the present amendment and move the one he had suggested.

The amendment was lost on a division of 39 to 34.

Mr. CRAWFORD moved, seconded by Mr. McDonald, (Gananoque), to expunge all after the words "The good of our common country," which was also lost.

Mr. GOWAN then moved his amendment, which was agreed to by Mr. Gamble and carried unanimously.

Mr. CRAWFORD then moved to strike out that part of the resolution which referred to the Montreal manifesto.

Mr. McDONALD, (Gananoque), seconded the motion. How could any gentleman stand up to argue on the question of Annexation after the Convention had agreed that the discussion of the question was the means of engendering "fierce political animosities."

Mr. ROLLAND McDONALD hoped the original resolution would carry. He did not wish it to be inferred from the way in which two or three gentlemen had spoken, that there was a large number of delegates present in favour of annexation; he thought there were few, if any, at present in favour of annexation, although there might be many who felt that if something was not done for us by Great Britain or ourselves, that we shall be driven into it as an unavoidable evil, not as a matter of choice. (Hear, hear.) He believed there were some who

thought that such a time was coming. With such he should be prepared to argue that the day might never come. God knows! he hoped he might never live to see it; if the majority of the people should turn to annexation and it should be brought about, he would sell his property and leave the country. (Hear, hear.) He would go to some other place where the British flag waves, and where there were people still to rally round it and bear it triumphantly on, "conquering and to conquer." He was not one of those who thought that the days of the British Empire were numbered yet. No! its high mission to civilize the nations was not yet accomplished. (Cheers.) Was he to be told that a country like Britain which extends her sway for the purpose of benefitting the human kind, was about tottering to its fall, while an Empire of quite an opposite nature, which traffics in human blood, was to flourish? He would never believe it. (Hear, hear.) He concluded by hoping that the amendment would be withdrawn.

The amendment was then put to the vote, and lost, and the Convention adjourned.

3 O'CLOCK, P. M.

After a desultory conversation, on the propriety of re-considering Mr. Crawford's amendment, which was objected to by Mr. G. T. Denison.

Mr. GOWAN rose and said, I exceedingly regret that the learned gentleman was not disposed to yield to the wishes of nine-tenths of the Convention, because, although I approve of the whole of Mr. Gamble's resolutions, with the exception of that which it was proposed to strike out; by his not yielding to the good sense of the majority, I am driven to the painful necessity of striking out the whole, and moving an amendment. I move that the whole of the resolution after the word "that" be struck out, and the following substituted—"this colony cannot continue in its present political or commercial state." As the question of annexation has been alluded to, I will take this opportunity of stating that there is not in this room a firmer Briton than him who now addresses you. Sir, I was born a Briton, and I hope and trust that I shall be enabled to die one; but, Sir, there can be no disputing the fact that annexation is rapidly gaining ground in this country. Let us not despise an enemy; let us admit his prowess, his numbers, and his adroitness, and we shall be better prepared and enabled to resist him when the time comes. If gentlemen think they are going to put down annexation by crying up—as has been done in some of the Government prints of the day—the state of the country as one of solid happiness and prosperity, they are laying a foundation of sand, on which the building must fall to ruin. Sir, a few years ago—a few months ago, I might rather say, to speak of annexation we should have looked upon as treason. (Loud cries of hear, hear.) Now, Sir, people meet in steamboats and hotels—we meet in this Convention—the newspaper press of the country —all parties meet now and discuss the question, without any reference to principle, but simply as a matter of £ s. d. Do we not then know by the progress it is making amongst ourselves—

by contrasting the present state of the question with what it was six—three—aye, even one month ago, that it is making rapid progress ? Who can dispute that point ? Sir, it is now, as I said, a matter of calculation—of £. s. d., not of principle. I have heard it asked, are you going to forego your principles—to put the question on the ground of £ s. d. ? Sir, I regret to state that that great country to which our allegiance is bound, has herself put the question on the principle of £ s. d. It is England that has told Canada, and not her faithful children in this distant dependency, that the question should be put on the ground of £ s. d. She has proclaimed in the whole of her Legislation that it is incompatible with the interests of her people, that we should enjoy the protection which from the first foundation of this, as a British Colony, we have enjoyed ; and in following her example, can gentlemen say we are acting in an unpatriotic manner. (Cheers.) Sir, annexation is a hard word for a Briton to pronounce—it is a hard word for me to pronounce, for, as I have already stated, I was born, a Briton, and hope to die one ; but there is something to be taken into consideration more than that. With me the love of Britain is a prejudice, but prejudice though it be, I must confess it has become with me a principle. (Hear, hear.) What do my resolutions propose ? I propose, in a subsequent resolution, if this be adopted, to go home to England, not of course myself individually, but that our excellent Chairman, or some other gentleman, should be delegated to go home, and to lay before that great nation, at the foot of the throne, the last appeal of the people of these Colonies for justice. (Loud cheers.) I would go to Lord Grey, the man who represents the power of England as it affects these Colonies. I would not threaten, it is true, but I would point to the road before him—a road that has been travelled before. I would tell Lord Grey to recollect that Benjamin Franklin was once sent to England from the thirteen Colonies of the Empire possessing, I believe, 1,300,000 white inhabitants. I would tell him to recollect that we have many more thousands than they had in this country, and I would say, my Lord, the people are yet loyal and true. I say not what the result of your refusal may be, but I ask you to read the past history of that disastrous event to the Empire of England. I would ask Lord Grey to accompany me to the shores of this country. I would tell him to come here, and not to be guided by the misrepresentations in the despatches of my Lord Elgin, but to come to British North America, and with his own eyes, with his own ears and with his own good sense to examine and decide on our present state. And now, Sir, what of our present state ? Suppose Lord Grey to come here—our first landing place would be at Halifax —we should sail up the beautiful bay, and first touch the shores of North America there. What would be the first thing his Lordship would behold ? We would wait upon one of the richest merchants of Halifax at St. John, or one of the eastern cities on the coast, and I would say,

look here, my Lord, here is the Province of Nova Scotia, on the left is New Brunswick, and on the right Newfoundland and Prince Edward's Island. These colonies of the Empire produce coal, timber and fish, and these are their sole articles of export. Here is a merchant holding, perhaps, twenty or thirty ships, and the country is one of unexampled extent and resources ; but you, by your policy, have allowed the ships of our American neighbours to come into our three or four ports on the same terms as our vessels ; they convey our coal, our timber and our fish to their ports, extending thousands of miles, on the same terms as ours, whilst we are obliged to get full cargoes to go into their ports. Therefore, when the American ship-owner comes into one of our ports and carries away our products, he can go to one of these ports and deposit a portion of his cargo there, take on board American produce, and convey it to the next port, and so go on to the gulf of Mexico, then round Cape Horn, and if he pleases, thence to the gold regions of California. The result is, that they come into our markets and bear away our produce at a cheaper rate than we can do. This would show to my Lord Grey the disastrous effect of his policy on the ship-building interests of the colonies. Next he would come up the River St. Lawrence to Quebec. What do we find there ? If we had happened to arrive three or four days ago, we should have found the capital of Lower Canada, the very Castle of St. Louis, shaken with the cheers of the inhabitants for annexation. (Hear, hear, hear.)— We should have found houses broken, a public meeting held, the resolutions frustrated by violence, and the people in the same state of violence and contention that characterised the sister city of Montreal some months ago. Sir, if the principle of annexation were adopted, what a premium would it not hold out to the great city of Quebec: perhaps no part of the continent of North America would be so much benefitted by annexation as Quebec. All who have any knowledge of the commercial transactions of this country and of the world, know that Quebec, from her proximity to the lumber, can afford, from having the material so near at hand, to furnish the materials for ship-building much cheaper than any other port in the world, and that labour at Quebec and generally through Lower Canada, is cheaper than in any other part of North America. Quebec then, from her proximity to the material, and the cheapness of labour, could afford to become the ship-building port of the world ; for even now she builds many ships for the trade of the Clyde, the Liffey, the Shannon, the Thames, and the Mersey—but what would she be then ? Let us travel next with Lord Grey to the Eastern Townships : take a trip to Sherbrooke,—what do you behold there ? You will find a farmer on one side of the lines and another on the opposite side : the farmer on the south side of the fence, with a climate no better, and with land no better, and sometimes inferior, if he desires to go to the Western States and sell his farm, he has only to give notice of his intention and he has immediately offers of 10, 20, or 30 pounds an acre for it, but if the man on the north side of the fence desires to sell his farm he must advertise, advertise, advertise, till by and by he may get £5 an acre for it. I would then ask, why this difference, why is it that a farm on the other side of the fence should be so much more valuable, so much more readily disposed of than the farm on this? I would ask my Lord Grey to explain it. I would ask him, is the farmer on the north side of the fence less industrious, less intelligent, less enterprizing, less laborious than his neighbour on the south side? Are his children better clothed—does he spend the product of his farm in extravagance? No, sir, on the other side you see better clothing, more comforts, equal intelligence, and certainly not more industry or hard labour. Then surely there must be some cause for it. I then ask his Lordship to come along by railroad from St John's to Montreal. What do we find there? The first object that strikes our attention after we land from the river is what is called ' the Elgin marbles ' (Hear) I have no desire to touch upon any political questions here, but as the matter has been referred to to-day, I will state exactly the view which I take of the burning of the Parliament House, so that there may be no misunderstanding regarding my opinion on that question ; some gentlemen have repudiated the act, none sanctioned it, but it occurred to me that I might compare the burning of the Parliament House to a friend whom I saw lying in the arms of death, having fallen in what is called an honourable duel ; we might lament and mourn over departed goodness and departed virtue, but we would forget the enormity of the crime in the insult that was the cause of it.— (Loud cheers.) Sir, having arrived in Montreal I would then say to his Lordship come with me through this great city—a few weeks ago the metropolis of British North America. What would we behold ? Sir, on every other house " to let," " to let," on every other corner, " *a louer,*" " *a louer,*" " Sheriff's sale," " Bankrupt sale," I would say then, my lord, here are the evidences of the prosperity of this country, there they are at every corner of the chief city of the Empire in British North America. I would then say, my lord, let us travel a little further ; you have been told the want of opportunity and depression of trade are confined to Lower Canada. Come let us have some personal observation of the effect on Upper Canada. We take the railroad, nine miles, from Montreal to Lachine, to take the steamboat, we find ourselves in the comfortable cars of the only railroad that has yet been made to connect the Upper and Lower Provinces together, and the stock of it is now at a discount of 80 per cent. Another evidence of our prosperity ! Well, we get on board the *Passport* or *Highlander*, and pass into Upper Canada. The first stopping place is Prescott. See, my Lord, these rotten wharves. This town had more evidence of prosperity and success twenty years ago than it has to-day. But cross the river to Ogdensburgh. Look upon this picture and upon that ! Behold the contrast. I need not attempt to draw it, for I presume that every gentleman here has seen both places. I would then come

up with his Lordship to Brockville, the place where I reside, and I must say that there are few people, if any, who have put their feet in that town, that have not said it was a lovely place indeed. He would behold our magnificent Court House, which the learned and excellent Chief Justice pronounced to be the first in the Province; he would behold buildings erected there not inferior to any in the city of Montreal ; large cut stone stores, of the finest masonry, and perhaps of the best architecture in the Province ; he would see streets clean and level, well macadamized— he would see broad plank walks on each side of the streets, where the ladies' white satin shoes would not be soiled, and he would say, what a prosperous and lovely place ! I would turn about and say to him,—my Lord, 'tis true nature has done much for us, and the intelligence and enterprise of the inhabitants have not been wanting in seconding the advantages which nature has conferred ; but my Lord, here in this great street, where are the farmers' waggons ? where are the steamers and schooners, carrying the products of the country and the merchandize from it ? Unfortunately they are not to be found. Here my Lord, is a ship-yard, which four years ago gave employment to hundreds of persons ; there is the proprietor Mr. Parker, he is an Englishman, but you have driven him to become an annexationist, while the hundreds to whom he gave employment in his ship-yard are seeking their livelihood in the States. This is the state in which we are placed in our part of the country. I might say a little more ; we have some inhabitants along our border—a border something like to the Niagara frontier—only divided by the river from the opposite side; many persons living on that border have been driven to cross the river, and smuggle for the necessaries of life from their families, and to sell to their neighbours articles which they cannot buy here on the same terms. Come, then, up to Kingston. What do we find there? Kingston, the great emporinm for the noble bay of Quinte, and a noble bay it is—a second Mediterranean—an inland sea, well settled and cultivated on both sides, and the only outlet they have is Kingston, and yet, with all these advantages, if it were not for the adventitious circumstance of Kingston having some military establishments there, it would be in a state little better than Prescott, but she has the advantage of these temporary military establishments, which, I understand, are about to be removed to this city. Well, sir, when we are in Kingston, I would ask His Lordship to take a walk with me into some of the establishments of Kingston—into the iron foundry for instance. What do we see ? We see poverty and destitution. We find that the Americans can bring their manufactured article into our market and compete with our people by paying 7½ per cent ; but if we go on the other side, we must pay 20 per cent, and the consequence is that our factories are deserted by those who have been useful artizans. We next come to Cobourg and Port Hope. Cobourg is no doubt a fine place ; there is the fine factory of Mr. Mackechnie there; an honour and a credit to the country, (cheers;) and as to Port Hope, I know no part of British North America so lovely and beautiful by nature as Port Hope. Well, sir, if we go into either of these places, we meet a number of good farmers from the back country, with produce from Peterboro', or Smith, or Manvers, or some of the back townships We find that if these persons could only deposit their produce on the opposite side, they would be getting 5s per bushel for their wheat, while they can only get 3s 6d per bushel on this side. We will suppose that one of these farmers has a surplus of 200 bushels of wheat to spare, after laying aside sufficient for the use of his farm; he loses on that the difference between 5s and 3s 6d, which on 200 bushels would be £15; and what is that? It is a tax on the farmer for maintaining the connexion.— (Cheers.) It is true that the *Globe* newspaper, of this city puts the question,—Are the farmers of Upper Canada going to sell their allegiance for the difference in the price of a paltry bushel of wheat? (Cheers.) Suppose I were to turn round and remind the *Globe*, that his political friends told us a few years ago, there never would be peace and tranquillity in this country so long as British domination in Downing-street existed. (Hear, hear, hear.) But now you tell us that you are ardently attached to " British domination " and " Downing-street influence," as you used to call it, that you are willing to sacrifice the difference in the price of a bushel of wheat; and that the loyalty of the brave men who turned out in 1837 and 8 to save this colony to the Mother country—of my gallant friend who occupies a seat within the bar, (Sir Allan McNab,) and those who turned out under him, was "spurious loyalty." After commenting at some length on the *Globe's* course with regard to the annexation question, and showing up the weakness of the arguments on the subject which have been put forth by that paper, Mr. Gowan continued—Sir, do you suppose that I have made all these comments to impress on this convention the necessity of adopting annexation? I do not; but I bring them forward, as I should do with Lord Grey, to show him the condition to which his policy has reduced this country. I would tell him—my lord, you must either alter this state of things yourself by our policy, or the alternative will come when you must allow us to alter it. (Cheers.) This state of things cannot be endured; and while I would not dictate to his lordship, yet I would say to him, our fathers in England have proved that they are too brave a people to be bullied; their blood mingling in our veins proves that their children will not be insulted. (Cheers.) I would tell his lordship that this state of things must alter, or they must prepare for the consequences, which poverty, ruin, and destruction must bring upon an injured people. (Cheers.) I think, therefore, I may safely say that all parties will agree with me that these colonies cannot continue in their present condition, either politically or commercially; and I desire that this fact which we have recorded before should be recorded again,

I desire that it should be sent home to England; that the state of this country should be fairly laid before the English nation, the English Parliament, and the English Sovereign. I desire to tell the Parent State that, though she has insulted us, though she has grievously injured us, still we can put up with that injury as the child receives the chastisement of the parent, but it may chastise too severely.— (Cheers.) I am not prepared by my resolutions to take on myself the responsibility of Annexation or Separation, and I desire that if that event should ever come about, that the responsibility of that act, nay more, that the odium of it should rest with the Mother Country, and not with us. I desire that the question should be fairly put before her; that she should be asked to do justice to her suffering children in Canada, and not that she should drive them as outcasts from the parental bosom; if she does so, our course is plain before us; we have a duty we owe to ourselves, to our children, and to our country; we cannot continue, in my opinion, as we are; we must have an altered condition of things; let it come when it may, come it must; it is impossible to suppose that a great and growing country like this can continue for any length of time to be governed by the mere stroke of the pen of the occupant of the Colonial Office for the time being; we must have a different course of policy, we must have a settled constitution and form of Government, we cannot go on in North America, as they have been doing in some parts of South America, having constant revolutions and changes; we must have something done, or else society will continue to be as it now is, shaken to its very foundation. He concluded by moving the amendment.

Mr. MURNEY (Belleville) seconded the amendment, but he could not agree in all that Mr. Gowan had said; he thought that he had taken Lord Grey through Canada and shown him the dark side of the picture only; he thought that there were marks of prosperity also, which might have cheered the heart of an Englishman like Lord Grey (hear, hear). He could hardly have passed through Upper Canada, without seeing our magnificent canals; but Mr. Gowan forgot to point out these works, unequalled on the continent, built by Canadian enterprize (hear, hear). He brought Lord Grey to Toronto, but he forgot to point out to him five banks, neither of which has ever yet failed; he forgot to show his lordship the Welland canal; he forgot to take him to Hamilton, and show him the prosperity of that city. Now, although the political atmosphere of Canada was very lowering, and although the men at the head of the government had driven the people to the very highest pitch of doubt in their own institutions and in the sincerity of the British government still to retain us; and though the government of England have treated with contempt the petitions sent home to them by the people of Canada, and raised the object of their indignation to the peerage, thereby adding insult to the injuries done the Canadians; yet still he believed that if the Conservatives of Canada would only work together for the general welfare, and pass it this Convention a moderate resolution, they might yet stem the torrent and persuade the people of England to adhere to their motto, " Ships, Colonies and Commerce." At the Kingston meeting, the very mention of annexation drew forth a universal burst of indignation, and the convention there was characterized by a spirit of anti-annexation. He had at first been of opinion that the question should be treated in the same manner at this convention; but as he had found it the wish of many gentlemen to bring the question up, he had yielded his opinion. His own opinion on the question was unchanged; he was opposed to annexation, and he thought that every remedy should be tried first. He believed that these were the views and feelings of the great majority of the convention; but he also thought that the people who signed the Montreal manifesto had found many warm sympathisers among gentlemen who were unwilling to express their opinions openly. Unless something is done speedily, the feeling that has manifested itself in Montreal will spread in Upper Canada. A few short months ago, the question was never mooted, until the passage of that unfortunate rebellion bill in Lower Canada, by which the loyalty of the people of this province was called "spurious"; by which the very men who saved the country in 1837-8, were taxed to pay the losses of the men they were then called upon to put down. It was after this that the question first became the subject of private conversation and then of public debate and controversy. He mentioned this to show that it was spreading more rapidly than they were perhaps aware of. He did hope the convention would take the matter up, and express their opinion honestly and fully; unless something were done at once, it would be impossible to stem the torrent (hear, hear).

Mr. WILSON (Quebec) rose for the purpose of opposing the amendment, and supporting the original resolution. Mr. Murney had made two or three remarks which he thought it necessary to notice, to clear the convention of a party character. Mr. Murney attributed the state of the country to the imbecility of the men now in power He (Mr. Wilson) could not agree with him in that; he believed that the present position of this colony arose from the legislation of the Imperial government, and not of the colonial; and if a comparison was to be drawn between the men now in power, and their predecessors, he should say that the present were the better of the two (cheers). Mr. Murney stated that he came to the convention with the same determination that he had when they last met together at Kingston—to put down annexation, and any approach to a discussion of that question. Had Mr. Murney and some of his friends acted with a little more wisdom at the last convention, they would have heard less of annexation at the present time;

if they had acted like prudent men, and allowed the questions to be discussed which he proposed should be discussed at that meeting, they would have heard nothing of annexation at this time; he was glad to hear that they had learnt wisdom (hear, hear). He (Mr. Wilson) would yield to no man in point of loyalty, but his loyalty was due to the interests of his country and his family; and if he found that his feelings were such, from birth and the associations of early childhood, that he could not live under a foreign flag, he would go to England, or some other part of the dominion of her flag; but he could not consent to remain in a country, when he conceived that the Imperial government was legislating against the interests of that country, and not condemn such legislation, simply because he wished to remain a British subject (hear, hear). No, the first duty he owed was to the land he lived in; and if it should be necessary that we should have any differences with Great Britain, he would not fail in the discharge of his duty to the province of Canada, if after all he found it necessary for the satisfaction of his own feelings to leave it (hear, hear). Many gentlemen had said that they would rather remain as they were, than hear of annexation; he would tell those gentlemen that unless Great Britain behaves differently, they will be driven to annexation (cries of " never—we'll die first"). Since he came here he had learned that the feeling in favour of annexation was gaining ground in Canada West, and it was absolutely necessary that they should take it up and discuss it as a matter of pounds, shillings and pence, for men will judge, according to their interests and not their attachments. He should support the original resolution, as he could not help thinking that the amendment was going to take the matter out of Mr. Gamble's hands.

Mr. MILLER was entirely opposed to the amendment, and he was very much surprised to hear Mr. Murney say, that a similar resolution was adopted at Kingston.

Mr. MURNEY was under the impression that there was such a resolution.

Mr. MILLER had no recollection of it. If one thing more than another would induce him to oppose the amendment, it was the tenor of the remarks by which it had been supported by Mr. Gowan, and the tenor of the resolutions of which it formed the first of the series. He was willing to agree with Mr. Gowan in every thing he had said about the condition of the Province, and he was prepared to go with that part of the amendment which said that the country could not continue in its present commercial state, but to say that politically the Province could not continue in its present state, was granting a position which he thought they would afterwards be sorry for. The political affairs of the Province are under our own control, and if they could not muster sufficient force to carry the elections at the polls, they should be content that their views were not carried out, instead of appealing to the Home

Government. And with regard to the commercial state of the Province, he thought that too was, to a certain extent, within our own controul; he would, therefore, oppose the amendment.

Mr. E. G. O'BRIEN could not see any reason because they disapproved of two or three words in it, for passing by Mr. Gamble's resolution, after the long discussion they had had on it. It appeared to him, that the gentleman who moved the amendment was more in favour of annexation than any thing else. (Hear, hear.) He had represented us not as a people able and willing to help ourselves if we had only fair play, but his object appeared to be, to shew us up as a people incapable of helping ourselves, and that, if by the policy of the Mother Country we should be cut off, we must inevitably fall into the very superior people across the lines. (Hear, hear.) He (Mr. O'B.) was one of those who did not think that this must follow. He doubted the superiority of the American people, and he doubted exceedingly the correctness of the view taken by Mr. Gowan of the condition of the country; true, Canada is suffering from depression, but then is it not notorious that the whole of Europe is likewise suffering from depression, and that the United States—thanks to British trade—are just recovering from great distress. If he (Mr. O'Brien) were to accompany Lord Grey to Halifax, he would say to him—Look round, here was once the great emporium of the West Indian trade—here is the place that bade fair to rival the first towns on the other side of the Atlantic, but your false policy, your free trade policy, has made it what it now is. But still the game is not up with old Halifax—he would point to the propellers and schooners from Toronto and Kingston, laden with American produce brought by British Canadian enterprize through British waters—the first instalment of a trade which bids fair to yield a large return. Then he would bring Lord Grey up the St. Lawrence, and he would point out to him the fishing grounds near Gaspe, and say, look at the rich mines of wealth which the false policy of England is preventing us from taking full advantage of. He would bring his Lordship to Quebec, where the red-cross banner of England floats, welcoming the emigrants to this new country where the same old flag still waves above their heads, and he would use the word of the Irish poet, and say:

"We tread the land that bore us,
The British flag waves o'er us,
Friends well tried are by our side,"

and, pointing across the lines, he would add,
"And the foes we hate before us."

(Cheers.) Over the ramparts of Quebec that flag still floats, the emblem of all that is good and righteous—that flag which has carried GOD's blessed Word to every corner of the world. And are we to quarrel with that flag because we are a little pinched in our means? He asserted, and he challenged contradiction,

that at this moment there is no nation on the face of the earth that stands so high for moral and intellectual worth, as Great Britain, or where the people are so imbued with religious feeling. Are these the people we are to cast off? In Montreal certainly a perambulating Government, and a great deal of misgovernment, had made a great many empty houses; but during the last ten years a great many houses had been built there, and the present state of the city was, in part, the consequence of over-speculation, but the Province generally was in a prosperous and flourishing condition.

Mr. A. J. McDONELL urged the propriety of at once coming to a vote, after all the time that had been lost in debating a resolution of comparatively little importance.

Mr. LANGTON thought the commercial as well as the political state of the Province should be taken into consideration, and he should therefore support the amendment.

Mr. HAMILTON did not see how the question of annexation came up on Mr. Gowan's amendment. He could not see beginning or end to Mr Gamble's resolution; he could not see that it attributed to any cause, much less to the right cause, the political agitation which exists, nor did it point out the remedy; it seemed to him to be a mere string of truisms put together without any definite object. Did any gentleman present mean to say, that the country could remain in its present political and commercial state—did any one maintain that? He had not come to the Convention to talk about the flag of Great Britain. He thought all that sort of thing was quite beside the question. He thought they should approach the subject with a statement of facts. Would any gentleman in his senses stand up and say, that with wheat at 3s. 6d. a bushel on one side of an imaginary line and 5s. on the other, that that was a state of things which the people would long bear? He thought that every person who looked at the present state of the country and took an interest in its welfare would say, that neither the political or commercial state of the country could long be endured by the people. Man is arrayed against man, the most bitter and rancorous feelings are pervading the length and breadth of the land. He did not think this was the proper time to discuss annexation—it was only opening up an immense field of discussion; if they were to do anything for the real good of the country, they must grapple at once with its present state—trace the evils under which it labours and suggest the remedy. It seemed to be admitted on all hands that we must go to England—look to British Legislation to alter the present state of affairs, If that be the case then upon what more sound tangible and sensible ground could they possibly base such an application, as on the ground that these colonies cannot longer continue in their present political or commercial state. If it be admitted that this is a fact, then the next question is, what has produced this state of things? He was not going to argue on the relative advantages of Great

Britain and the United States—there could be no question concerning the relative prosperity of this country and the United States—the subject would not admit of argument—it was plain palpable to every one. He did not wish to have the question of Annexation burked as it was at Kingston, they must grapple with it and make England feel that she has to do with a people who feel their own position and strength, and will not be trampled on or insulted. (Cheers) It was possible that representations made from this colony might lead to some result, but he had never seen any good come of the various representions that had been made to England and the deputations sent home. The Convention might rest assured that it was impossible for the question of a change to be now stifled. It was difficult to reach the farmers on mere political questions, but the question of the depressed state of the country touches this 80 per cent. of the population, and they will not long allow the remaining 20 per cent. to interfere with or stifle their best interests. The eagerness with which the Convention had plunged into the question of Annexation, proved what a hold it had already taken in the country

Mr. GAMBLE replied to some remarks made by the speakers against his resolution. One gentlemen had objected to the resolutions because they did not relate in any way to the commercial state of the country He (Mr. G.) had no intention that they should relate to the commercial interests of the country; these matters were taken up at the last meeting of the Convention, and he could see no possible benefit to arise from the Convention reiterating the same thing over again. At the former meeting the Convention had discussed these matters, and he was now introducing political discussion because he proposed certain changes in our constitution as a remedy for some of the evils under which we suffer. The Convention after mature consideration, agreed upon Protection, Retrenchment, and a union of the Provinces, as the best remedy for the evils of the country, and it was now for them to adopt steps to carry out those views.

Mr. GEO. DUGGAN rose amidst loud cries of " question," he rose for the purpose of suggesting that in order to secure unanimity, the resolution and amendment should be referred to a Committee to embody them so as to meet the views of all. He thought there was not much difference of opinion with regard to the state of the country and the remedy ; and with regard to the question of annexation he thought that was the grand question to be brought forward, if they intended to produce any impression on Great Britain; we must shew them the impending danger to the country ; we must shew them that the farmers will not consent to be taxed £100,000 for the connection. He desired that Great Britain should understand that the people of this colony know their own interests, and have the spirit of British freemen, and will not allow any Government—no matter what its name—to deprive them of their rights—that they will contend for them in a proper spirit, and will not be satisfied with less than as British freemen they are entitled to—let the people of England understand that this Colony claims from England their rights—they ask nothing from England that England would not take from them, but neither will they be satisfied with anything less from England than they consider themselves fairly and honestly entitled to—let them come manfully to the point, and then they might hope to move England. Let them tell her that the rebels of Lower Canada have been paid, that the loyalists of the country have been outraged, and that the Parliament houses have been burned down in consequence, and what would be the result? they would tell us, as the Colonial Secretary told Sir Allan McNab, that he hoped he would preach up peace and quiet to the people, that there was very little cause for discontent in the country; and that he was sorry for the riots in Montreal. Was this a proper answer to be given—were the representations on these great and important matters to be treated with contempt—would they stand this treatment ? He for one never would ! He concluded by moving that the resolution and amendment be referred to a special Commitee.

After a somewhat desultory conversation it was determined that the Convention should adjourn till 7 o'clock, to give Messrs Gowan and Gamble an opportunity of preparing a resolution that would meet the views of both parties.

7 O'CLOCK, P. M.

Mr. *Gowan* asked for and obtained leave to withdraw his amendment to Mr. Gamble's resolution.

Mr. *J. W. Gamble* asked for and also obtained leave to withdraw his resolution.

Mr. *J. W. Gamble* moved, seconded by *Mr Gowan*, that it be

Resolved,—That the condition of this Province calls loudly upon all lovers of peace and good government, speedily to adopt measures whereby the present excitement may be allayed, public tranquillity restored, and existing political differences merged in one paramount sentiment—the good of our common country. For some time past, disturbance has followed disturbance, and riot has succeeded riot in quick succession ; on several occasions human blood has been shed, the law violated with impunity, while the Government, by their ineffectual attempts to repress these disorders, have been brought into contempt. Exciting and irritating political questions, involving the dismemberment of this Colony from the Empire, are openly advocated. Rancorous feelings are separating neighbour from neighbour, to the hindrance and neglect of business, the interruption of industry, the loss of confidence, and the destruction of credit. The public mind is becoming vitiated by these excesses, a spirit of insubordination to the laws is manfested, which if allowed to prevail, threatens to burst asunder the bonds of society, and lead to the most deplorable consequences—anarchy, confusion, and civil strife ; and that for these and other causes, it is the opinion of this Convention that these Colonies cannot continue in their present political or commercial state.

Which was carried.

Mr. *J. W. Gamble* then moved, seconded by Mr. *Wilson*, that it be

Resolved,—That in order to assuage the present excitement and discontent, to prevent collision between our fellow subjects, to promote union among all, and to determine the great political questions now agitating the public mind, in accordance with public opinion, it is necessary that the feelings, sentiments opinions the people should be faithfully represented in the Legislative Assembly at its next Session; which can only be attained by the exercise of the Royal Prerogative in the dissolution of the present Parliament and the summoning of a new one.

Mr. GAMBLE argued that the present depression of provincial trade was entirely occasioned by the varying commercial policy of England. The Indemnity Bill was not the cause of the excitement which had existed, and still exists; it was but the spark applied to the train. The Provincial Ministry was entirely pledged to free-trade; it was useless to appeal to them; there was but one course left. which was to petition the Governor to dissolve the House, for the purpose of ascertaining the sense of the people. If the country goes with us, the question will be decided; if not, he for one was ready to submit to the will of the majority.

Mr. WILSON, (Quebec), supported the resolution.

Dr. HAMILTON was of opinion that a dissolution would produce no beneficial results.

Mr. R. McDONALD (St. Catherines,) thought the present time a very improper one to hold a general election From what had taken place in our principal cities, on the occasion of Lord Elgin's visit, there could be no doubt that a general election would produce serious disturbances. He would rather see the ministry remain in office; they would soon destroy themselves by their own measures.

COL. FRASER was opposed to a dissolution, as was also Mr. AIKMAN.

Mr. A. J. McDONELL said it would be quite useless to petition the real Governor of the province—Mr. Lafontaine—for a new election; the ministry would never consent to deprive themselves of their own salaries.

Mr. G. DUGGAN was not disposed to petition Lord Elgin for anything, (hear, hear,) it was useless to do so. He would oppose the motion. He could not forget that the earnest and respectful petitions of many thousands of the people of this country had already been treated by Lord Elgin with utter disregard and indifference. He considered that the country was prepared for a general election, the people felt sensitively alive to the grievances under which they laboured, and if an opportunity were afforded them, they would displace the men who now mis-governed the country, and brought it to its present distracted condition. But it was idle to petition Lord Elgin with his present advisers,—petition to be insulted! By the partizan course of the Governor-General, even our Representatives in Parliament could not escape, they had been singled out in the House and their characters and conduct animadverted upon. and what would be thought of a ministry at home who should advise the Queen to animadvert upon particular members of the House of Commons? This course was reserved for the present ministry as a resort for themselves through Lord Elgin. But mark the fruits of his Excellency's presence in different parts of the country. What are they? They are bloodshed and strife and calamity. Witness the loss of human life at Bytown, the triumphal arches erected by one party and torn down by

another, and the excitement pervading the community from Quebec to London. His presence is felt as a blight and by many a loyal man a curse to the country. No such state of things was ever before brought about amongst us. The public feeling of the country had never before been so greatly outraged, the thing was without a parallel, and language such as was not heard towards the Representative of the Sovereign, expressive of indignation and contempt was now heard undisguised as common conversation in our streets. Our course should be to place before the people our opinions of what was necesssary for the good of the country. He would ask the farmers would they consent to pay upwards of one hundred thousand pounds a year as a tax on their produce, and which they now were paying this year. They would all understand this part of it whether reformers or tories. He would, by all means, ask for a dissolution of Parliament, if it could be obtained, the people were ready for it. But, Sir, it would not be granted to them. The ministry were bent on carrying out a different policy than the one we seek; they will treat with contempt your petitions for a dissolution. They treated with contempt the Legislative Council of the Province when that body after being invited to express an opinion as to the Seat of Government, gave their opinion. But which being unsuited to the wishes of the ministry both they and the Governor-General treated as a nullity, and not wishing to face the country at present, they will treat your petitions with contempt.

Mr. E. G. O'BRIEN did not think any serious disturbances were to be apprehended from a general election. There might be a few broken-heads perhaps, as there often had been. He believed however that the better way would be to lay information before the country, and to call for a better construction of the Legislative Council. He was no party man; if the ministry would mend their ways, he should never oppose them. (Hear, hear.) Some of them were called amiable men—why, the French revolution had been commenced by some of the most amiable of men. Like all reformers, they were cold, heartless theorists.

Mr. GAMBLE said, among the evils of this country, one of the greatest was legislation by lawyers; (hear, hear); some of the arguments he had heard seemed to prove it, for they were all for delay. He wanted to know the opinion of the country—if they were against us, he would submit; if not, we shall get what we want. He was sorry to hear abuse of the ministers; language like that, of a party character, would weaken our influence, and tend to shake the confidence of the country.

Mr. VANKOUGHNET warmly defended the legal profession; he was ready to admit, and had often stated his opinion, that the worst laws of this province had been carried through by lawyers. He questioned the propriety of passing the resolution. Were he Mr. Baldwin, he should adopt the course pointed out by the resolution, by dissolving the House of Assembly; there never would be so favorable an opportunity.—The resolution did not point out any object to be obtained.

[Mr. Gamble here contradicted the speaker, and some warm remarks passed.]

Mr. GAMBLE was ready to apologize if he had spoken too abruptly. The objects of the League had been already declared—they were, Protection, Retrenchment and Union; the object of the present resolution was to carry out those great principles.

Mr. VANKOUGHNET repeated that there was nothing in the resolution referring to any remedies for the evils under which the country suffered. If carried out, by a dissolution, the only effect would be, to secure the ministry in their seats for the next four years. He considered that sufficient had not been done to place the principles of the League fully before the country.

Mr. GOWAN said there were two reasons why he was not disposed to adopt this resolution; the first was, that we had already petitioned, and our petitions had not been forwarded home, although others had : the second, for the reason that Lord Elgin gave for assenting to the Rebellion-losses bill—that the majority of the house was with him. We should stultify ourselves by asking for the same thing a second time. A meeting was held in the Johnstown District, at which the sheriff and a number of the leading reformers were present, and an address against the Rebellion-losses bill was adopted, of which his Excellency has never even acknowledged the receipt.

Mr. R. McDONALD supposed our petitions were detained in order to give them due consideration.

Mr. DIXON thought the resolution premature; he would move that its consideration be postponed.

After a few words from other Speakers, Mr. Gamble consented to withdraw his resolution, reserving to himself the right of bringing it up at a subsequent period.

The motion was withdrawn.

SATURDAY MORNING, Nov. 3rd.

MR. GAMBLE moved his third resolution, seconded by Mr. John Young, of Hamilton, as follows :—

Resolved—That while the three remedial measures, Protection, Retrenchment and Union, held forth by the British American League, are manifestly those best calculated to effect the desired change, and restore prosperity to our drooping interests, it is equally apparent that those measures cannot be carried into successful operation, the necessary reforms accomplished, and a just, wise, and cheap system of government established, without important alterations in our constitution, requiring joint and concerted action with our sister Provinces. To this end it is expedient to obtain the authority of the Legislature, for holding a General Convention of Delegates, for the purpose of considering and preparing, in concert with Delegates from those Provinces, a new constitution, to be afterwards submitted for ratification to the people of Canada, and of such of the other Colonies as may decide upon acting in unison with them, preparatory to its being brought under the consideration of the Metropolitan Government.

At their former meeting the convention, after considering the various causes that led to the depressed state of the interests of the province, and the remedies that most prominently presented themselves, determined that they were these : protection to native industry, retrenchment in the public expenditure, and a union of the British North American provinces. In those measures he most heartily concurred ; he believed then as he believed now, that if these measures were properly and efficiently carried out, they would accomplish the objects the convention had in view, and bring the country into such a state of prosperity, that when we look on the other side of the lines we shall see nothing to envy. The convention having done that, it seemed to him a proper course for them to pursue on the present occasion, to show the people the way in which these remedies can be carried out ; it was with that view that he moved the resolution, subsequently withdrawn ; he trusted, however, that on reflection the members of the Convention would see the propriety of re-considering that resolution, and adopting it. He thought that the proper course to pursue would be, to endeavour to have their views reflected in the Legislature. If public opinion did not coincide with their views it was useless at present endeavouring to enforce them,—he, for one, had no desire to adopt other than constitutional means to attain that end ; the good of the country was the sole object he desired, he had no selfish ends to gratify,—office was no consideration with him, he cared not a straw about it ; and though he had discharged many public trusts and duties during his life, he had never held an office of profit or emolument, and he did not suppose he ever should, but what he desired was, that he and those like him who had nothing to do with the laws but to obey them, might not be disturbed in their avocations by the bickerings of party, and that the laws might be such as to prevent one party when in power from wreaking their vengeance on the party out of power. Since the last Convention he had spoken with a large number of people on the state of the country, and as to what they thought the best means to restore its prosperity ; he had consulted many persons of the soundest judgment and strongest minds, and had been told with few exceptions, that the true remedy for our evils is, the establishment of manufactures. You must get manufactures before the country can prosper, and that being his own conviction he felt his previous opinion greatly strengthened. The next thing to enquire is, how are we to obtain these manufactures? You cannot obtain them without protection. The only way in which you can establish manufactures in a young country, exposed to competition with foreign countries where manufactories have been established for ages, is by placing such a heavy duty on the articles you manufacture as will shut out the foreign article. Without the aid of a high tariff it is impossible for beginners to compete successfully with the experience, the skill, the minute division of labour, and the capital of those countries, where manufactures have long been domesticated. It was contended by the advocates of annexation, that even if we had protection it would not effect all the objects sought. He would admit that protection will not produce the changes we desire at once—it would not pay overdue bills, neither would annexation; you cannot say—change, pass, begone, and the thing is accomplished, but protection will produce a state of affairs that will soon result in prosperity ; because, when people find that their labour is profitably and liberally rewarded, they will be induced to turn their capital into those channels from which the greatest returns are obtained.— You will encourage the artizan to take up his abode among you and increase his business, because then he will find he makes more money by it here than elsewhere : you will stimulate labour by largely rewarding it, and then it is astonishing how rapidly a change takes place in every interest in agriculture and commerce as well as in manufactures. They acted and reacted upon each other : he showed from statistical returns the manner in which the rapid increase of manufactures in England during the latter part of the last century had stimulated agriculture ; from 1760 to 1834, every 100 increase in the population added 68 acres to the cultivated lands—while if the calculation be confined to the first twenty-five years of the present century, the proportion is only thirty-seven acres to every hundred. Such was the effect in England, and similar results may fairly be anticipated here. He for one, did not hold to the idea, that large sums of money were to be made on capital accumulated by working solely with borrowed capital ; he believed that to prosper, we must accumulate capital by our own labour and industry, and adopt such a policy as will not only reward labour well and tend to the accumulation of capital, but, after it is accumulated, will keep it where it is accumulated. Borrowing capital, especially from foreign countries, must not be looked upon as a good without alloy to the country that borrows it. For instance, look at the large loans contracted in England for the completion of our public works ; the interest on that money is so much every year subtracted from the capital of the country ; that is the view taken in England, and the financiers there understand it. It was only the other day he read an article in an English paper, calling attention to the large amount of English stocks held by foreigners, and pointing to the consequences as prejudicial, and not contributing to the prosperity of the community. If we borrow capital, the profit derived from that capital must go out of the country ; the interest on the money borrowed to finish our canals goes to England. A large quantity of bank stock is held in England, and thither flows the profits of banking on such capital ; then come the life assurance offices of English companies, like a sponge, to suck up the little that may be left, and take it out of the country. If we desire to prosper, we must shut out the manufactures of foreign nations, and import the

mechanics that make them, to consume in the country our agricultural produce. Then we should prosper. He could assure gentlemen that it would not take a long time—a few years would suffice—to bring about a different state of things from that which we see at present. From the first British legislation for Canada, we never had a policy calculated to benefit the interests of this country ; the interests of the country never had been consulted. He had before him some of the statutes passed. The first act to regulate the trade of the province to which he would refer; was the 14th Geo. III., which imposed certain duties on foreign spirits, as distinguished from British, imported into this colony. For whose benefit was this law enacted ? Not for the benefit of the people of this country, nor was that advanced by paying 6d. a gallon more for spirits because it came from a foreign country instead of Great Britain. The law was enacted to foster the trade of England, to protect the carrying-trade of Great Britain, without any regard had to our interest. Look, then, at the British Possessions Act. That act imposed a duty of 20 per cent. on sugar, the produce of or refined in foreign countries. For whose benefit was it that we had to pay 20 per cent. for foreign silk and glass manufactures, while British articles of the same description paid a duty of 2½ only ? It was to secure to Great Britain the supplying us with those articles. Next we find a duty of 15 per cent. on all oils, the produce of foreign fisheries. For whose benefit was this ? Was it not for the purpose of encouraging the fishery trade of Great Britain ? But to come down to later times—the repeal of the corn laws, the supposed cause of all our troubles. In 1825, the legislature of Great Britain passed an act, admitting the importation of grain from Canada at a fixed duty of 5s. per quarter. In 1841, an agitation was commenced in Canada, to accomplish the free admission of our flour and grain into Great Britain. Gentlemen might remember the petitions to the Queen and the Imperial legislature, that were signed by almost all from one end of the province to the other. It was in Lord Sydenham's time, and he forwarded the movement. In 1843, we obtained our request ; but was it obtained because it was thought necessary for us, as likely to benefit us ? —or had our interests anything to do as a procuring cause of that measure ? No such thing. It was granted because Sir Robert Peel felt that it was necessary to adopt some other system against the future, besides that adopted in the modified corn bill of 1842, that the grain of the western States of America might be introduced through the " back door of Canada," as it was styled by Mr. Cobden. It was not done with a view to our benefit, but to meet their own particular emergency ; they felt that it was necessary to let food into England in some way, and they thought this a good one, and they invited us to join in it. Two or three years after , they determined to do away with the corn laws altogether—did they consult our interests then? —did they do us common justice ? He would

ask any gentleman acquainted with the transactions of that period, if they did us common
justice ? Was it not perfectly competent for
Sir Robert Peel, at the same moment that he
did away with that protection on our products,
to have done away also with the distinctive duties here in favour of British manufactures ?
But whilst our produce had no protection in the
British market, these duties remained in force
here, until the Canadian legislature at last repealed them. Common justice required, that
when the corn laws were repealed, they should
have repealed these distinctive duties also,
and he would go further and say the Navigation Laws as far as related to our sea-
ports. [Mr. Gamble then read an extract
from an article in the London Economist,
admitting that the British Government had been
guilty of a breach of faith on the occasion he referred to; that Canada had contracted a debt to
build the St. Lawrence Canal on the faith that
protection would be continued. It was all very
well after this to talk about " the fostering Legislation of the Imperial Government." That he
believed was the phrase, used in the Address
adopted at the last Convention, which he had
the honor of reporting from the Committee, although he disapproved of the expression. To
him these acts appeared not the fostering legislation of a wise Imperial Government, but the
acts of an unnatural parent whose intense selfishness has beggared her offspring. (Cheers.)—
The great mistake which has been made in this
country and which tends to lessen its produc-
tions, is forcing too much labour into one channel. The particular channel into which labour
has been thrust is the production of wheat; we
produce more wheat in proportion to our numbers than other people, and the consequence is
that the whole production of the country is
wonderfully diminished. In support of this he
would just refer to statistics published by authority. The whole production of wheat in the
United States in the year 1847 was 114,245,500
bushels, or 5 bushels and 50 parts to each inhabitant. At the same time in 1847 the quantity of wheat produced in Canada was 7,558,773
or 10 bushels and 45 parts to each inhabitant.
This was vaultingly put forward, as shewing that
Canada, in proportion to its extent and population, was a more agricultural country than the
United States, and could export one half the
produce yielded by its soil. Now mark the result of thus forcing our people to become agri-
culturists—growers of wheat. That same year,
1847, the whole quantity of grain and potatoes
grown in the United States was 46 bushels and
$\frac{72}{100}$ for each inhabitant, while in Canada it was
only 32 bushels and $\frac{69}{100}$ for each inhabitant.
Many, many were the evils that flowed from
this system of compelling people, whether fitted
or not for the employment, to become farmers.
The artizan on reaching Canada, finding no employment in that pursuit to which he has been
brought up, either leaves the country for the
States or attempts to farm; ignorant of agriculture, and unaccustomed to farm labour, his
utmost exertions fail in procuring sufficient for

himself and family; little by little his means
decrease, till, having exhausted all he brought
with him, discouraged and desponding, he too
frequently becomes a drunkard, then an inmate
of the gaol and Penitentiary, unless indeed lu-
nacy or premature death anticipate that event.

We have ample means of becoming wealthy,
and independent, but capital will not accumulate with us without manufactures. The reason
is plain. The material used in cotton and wool-
en manufactures doubles and trebles in value
from the time it leaves the hand of the producer
till it is returned to him in the shape of cloth.
The quantity of cotton consumed by the British
manufacturers in 1847, estimated by McCulloch,
was 500,000,000 of pounds, costing in Britain
$45,000,000, for which the planter received
$35,000,000; four-fifths of this was American.
The value of British cotton manufacture in
that year was £42,000,000; and the number
of operatives employed 540,000. The amount
of capital employed and the annual product is
estimated to be about the same. This shews,
that after deducting the cost of the material, the
manufacturer produced $115,000,000 worth of
goods, or $266 per hand. The planter with an in-
vested capital of $170,000,000 and 250,000 hands
produced $35,000,000, or $140 per hand, shewing
that producing the material yielded $122 per
hand less per annum than manufacturing it. He
had made a similar calculation from data obtained in the Provincial Statistics, which shew-
ed that while the average product of each hand
employed in agriculture for the year 1847 was
about £22 14s. 6d., that of the wool-manufac-
turing operatives was at the rate of £126 15s per
hand. Having said this much, he should now pass
on to the question of a union of the Provinces, and
before entering into the subject itself he would
say a few words with regard to the report of
the meeting of Delegates in Montreal, that had
been laid on the table last evening, and for which
considerable blame was thrown upon some one :
he (Mr. G.) did not deny that blame existed,
but he would take the opportunity of saying
that none of it belonged to him, although he was
one of the committee appointed at the Kingston
Convention. It would be recollected that at
the time he strongly urged upon the gentlemen
to whom the matter was entrusted, the absolute
necessity of writing to New Brunswick, Nova
Scotia and the other provinces, to obtain all the
statistical information possible, in order that
they might have something to act upon ; he
urged that the Delegates from the other provinces should be requested to bring such statistics
as they could get of their trade, resources, and
other matters which should have formed part of
the report now laid on the table. From the time
he left Kingston he heard nothing of the meeting of Delegates till he received a notice on the
evening of the 10th of Oct., that the meeting
was to take place on the 12th. He immediately
set out, and reached Montreal on the morning
of the 13th, when the meeting was over ; the
gentlemen did him the kindness to re-assemble
and talk the matters over, but they had agreed
to the propositions that had been submitted to

the Convention, and he (Mr. G.) assented also after hearing them read, but was not satisfied that the matter should end there. He went down prepared to see what arrangement could be made, but he found that the gentlemen from New Brunswick had no authority to agree to anything. He for one could not see any insurmountable difficulty in carrying out such a union as that proposed, a federal union, but he could see vast benefits that would arise to all parties out of a close and intimate union. These provinces might form the nucleus of a great and mighty nation. When he looked to the vast extent of territory, and natural resources that the connection would give us, the inexhaustible treasures of coal, the fisheries and timber of the other provinces, he was convinced that nothing but a wise system and policy was necessary to make us a great and prosperous people, and if we could only draw closely around us the bands of union, we should soon be enabled to stand on our own feet, and maintain our position and rights among the nations of the world. He would carry out the proposed union on the very principle on which the new Municipal Act is based—that same act alluded to and condemned by two gentlemen of the Convention as uncalled for and useless ; those gentlemen, however, had admitted never having read it—the same act that, when notice was given of it in the Legislature, he himself, with the rest of the Council of this District, had declared against, as not required by the people, and which he feared as emanating from those deemed visionaries, and impracticable—that same act, having now closely examined, he felt convinced was the greatest boon ever conferred upon Canada by its Legislature—it was based upon the great principle of concentration as opposed to centralization, the foundation of good and lasting government ; a government that could never break down, because it would be rooted in the hearts of the people ; the power of governing their own local affairs is fully conceded to the people by that act. Although he believed it to be a little in advance of the times here, he was satisfied that nothing but good could redound from it.— This was the principle on which he would base the proposed union, and he would state to the Convention, as briefly as possible, the general outline of the plan upon which he proposed to accomplish it. The act he had mentioned found the people of this Province desirous of associating in little communities for purposes in which all were interested, and it gave them the power to associate for those purposes : enter, for instance, one of the farm-houses in the township from which he came, and what will you find there ? The owner of the household turning his eyes inwards ; his wife, his children, his farm, his cattle, and his house stand first in his thoughts, in these he finds his happiness ; but if from what appeared such selfishness we conclude that man incapable of associating with his fellows, because his thoughts were concentrated upon home, we would be greatly mistaken ; he discusses with his immediate neighbours the laying out and improving of roads, the institu-

tion of schools, required by his children, the arrangement of the little village, and the necessary contributions for those purposes : then he combines with more distant neighbours for maintaining roads he sometimes uses, the support of grammar schools, the maintenance of security to person and property, the settlement of differences, and the regulation of matters of general interest, by which he may at times be affected. First, there is the home, then the home of the little community, then the home of the several communities—two more sweeps of the circle, each time with increased diameter, and you have the home of the Province, and then the home of several Provinces ; with each step the tendency to union will be found to spread. In the event of a federal union, Canada might be divided into three Provinces—East, Central, and West Canada ; then we should have New Brunswick, Nova Scotia, Newfoundland, and Prince Edward Island in all 7 provinces, united in one confederacy. Such an union he felt satisfied would contribute to the welfare of the whole, and enable us at the same time to continue the connexion with Great Britain, and have the British flag still waving over us. Each province should exercise sovereign power within itself, except in those cases where it is expressly specified. With Great Britain should remain the power of legislating on those subjects, which concern the honour of the Empire, namely, allegiance to the Crown, treaties with any foreign power, commercial treaties excepted, political intercourse between any foreign power and the Colony, employment, command and discipline of her Majesty's troops, and ships within the Colony, and defence of the Colony from foreign aggression, including the command of the militia and marine in time of war, and whatever relates to the crime of high treason. To the confederation he would cede the power to levy duties, which duties should be uniform throughout the confederation, and be divided among the several provinces in proportion to the amount payable upon the articles subject to such duties imported into each respectively—to borrow money on the credit of the confederation —to regulate commerce with Great Britain, foreign nations, and among the several provinces—to establish uniform laws of naturalization and of bankruptcy—to coin money, regulate its value and that of foreign coin—to provide for the punishment of counterfeiting the coin or securities of the confederation—to fix the standard of weights and measures—to establish post offices and post roads—to provide for the issuing of patents—to provide for the punishment of piracies and felonies committed on the high seas, and offences against the law of nations—to provide for calling out the militia to execute the laws of the confederation and suppress insurrection—to make regulations affecting emigrants from Great Britain and foreign countries, and to impose a tax thereon—legislate on all subjects relating to the internal communication of Canada, by its lakes, rivers and canals, and to establish a tribunal for the decision of questions arising from alleged infringements

B

of the rights reserved to either party, somewhat similar to the Supreme Court in the United States. These matters provided for, he could see no difficulty about the plan—each part of the confederation would be able to make its own laws, to carry out its own views, and pursue the course it deems most for its interest, with Free Trade between all the provinces. A union of this kind would leave the people nothing to desire from annexation, because, in a few years, this country would be in quite as prosperous a state as the other side of the lines; by this means we should be secured from that which is no longer to be endured, Downing Street rule; whether it was want of inclination or want of knowledge, the results to us were alike, our interests were neglected, the ignorance of the Colonial Office was proverbial—it was not an affair of yesterday. He remembered an anecdote, recorded before he was born:—An English gentleman desired to introduce his nephew at the levee of a Minister of the Crown, in the reign of George the Second, the Duke of N——. On arriving he found the duke not yet risen.— The company were received by a Captain C., a sort of half spy, half attache. That gentleman amused them by running down his employers. Since they turned out Grenville, he said, England had not had a Minister worth the meal that powdered his periwig—they are so ignorant there is no making them comprehend the simplest proposition. As for this numskull, the best thing he can do is to sleep on till Christmas. It was only the other day that he came running to me—my dear C., have you heard the news? What news? The French have marched 30,000 men from Nova Scotia to Cape Breton. Where did they get the transports? Transports, I tell you they marched by land. By land to the Island of Capt Breton! What! is Cape Breton an island? I pointed it out to him on the map. Egad, I'll in and tell the King Cape Breton's an island.— (Cheers and great laughter.) He now came to what would perhaps have obtained little favour three months ago. He entertained the same opinions as to the constitutional changes he was about to propose then that he did now; but he saw a greater reason for these opinions being carried out now, because the annexation movement has greatly progressed since the Convention last met. If this scheme of union were carried out, he should propose a great constitutional change in our Government. He said constitutional, because it would affect the appointment of two of the legislative bodies, so as to adapt them to the circumstances of the times. He supposed he should be met at the outset by that sort of thing which they had heard before in this Convention—that no kind of change ought to be permitted, because when changes once begin there is no knowing where they may end. He would be opposed, doubtless, by that extreme admiration for existing institutions that can see no fault, and that acute sensibility that can endure no change. But he would ask these gentlemen what was the course of mankind in all things? Are we not going on,

going on, perpetually advancing in improvement? Is not our course onward—onward still? And are those portions of our laws, termed the constitution—the constitution of the country—to be the only things to remain stationary? He imagined that, in former ages, men adapted their institutions very much to their circumstances. He believed that when knight errantry was the order of the day, it was very well adapted to the circumstances of the times, but is it calculated for these times? So the feudal system was well calculated for the purpose for which it was intended, viz., to protect property from the attacks of marauders, but does that answer the circumstances of our age? Are not a portion of the people of Canada oppressed by this system and desirous of throwing it off? The legislation with regard to the constitution of the country, like everything else must be progressive, it should be associated with progress; that great principle which has been defined by the most eloquent of men as the noblest item in the charter of the privileges of human nature, who has said that it is that same principle which belongs to us in our affinity with heaven—that it raises us to a higher grade of being—that it infuses into us a oneness with that being who rules every where, educing good from evil, and making that good more vast and more lasting; that principle that appeals only to our best powers, that is allied with our brightest prospects; that has in it a tendency to make man worthy of the position he occupies on earth, and not unworthy of having within him a principle of enduring life, for which ampler spheres, and noble enjoyments and occupations are provided. [Cheers.] To this description of progress, as a principle of action, his heart and soul, every feeling within him responded; and those gentlemen who would confine us to the present system, and seek to establish a sort of fixed standard from which we must never depart, are at variance with human nature. We must make those changes which the circumstances of the times call for. Now, one of the first of these changes is such a one as will identify the person at the head of the Government with the interests of the country. [Loud cries of hear, hear.] How are we at present circumstanced? We have a stranger sent out to us from a distant land; he comes here ignorant of the circumstances of the country, and of what is wanted, he has every thing to learn; he remains here a few years, and if he is industrious and desirous of studying the wants of the people, he is sent to govern, he will, after three or four years, have accumulated the necessary knowledge to enable him to acquire a proper understanding of our circumstances; when three or four years have elapsed he is ordered home and replaced by another stranger. [Loud cries of hear, hear.] He would ask was that consistent with common sense and reason? [Cheers.] Then, according to the present system, the Governor is unaccountable, and is to do nothing himself. He [Mr. Gamble] proposed to have a man elected from among ourselves, and instead of giving him $30,000 per annum, he would give him $2,000, and he should have the veto power, with proper restrictions, like some of the Governors on the other side of the lines; he should have the same means of checking the power of legislating under sudden ebullitions of popular feeling, which might afterwards be regretted. The next reform he would propose would be an elective Legislative Council. [Cheers.] He [Mr. Gamble] did not believe in the divine right of Kings to appoint Legislative Councillors any more than in the divine right of constables; the circumstances of the country made a reform of the kind necessary. The Legislative Council, as at present constituted, is not an independent branch of the Legislature, and his object was to make it so. He wished this branch of the Legislature to be secured due deliberation, to have a Conservative tendency; for while he desired to go forward and progress with the spirit of the age, he also desired that that spirit might be kept from running rampant by those checks common to free institutions. That was the object he sought to acquire, and they who agreed with him would go for an elective Legislative Council. [Cheers.] There were other reforms much needed—those of finance were not the only ones required, and none more so than with regard to the legal profession. [Hear, hear.] For a long period, a large proportion of the Legislature has been composed of the members of that profession, and they have hedged it round in such a way as to form a perfect monopoly; they have appropriated large sums of the public money for the purpose of benefitting those at the head of the profession, that when their members have got worn out in the service, they may have a comfortable shelf, on which to recline, with twelve to fifteen hundred a year; then they have extended their privileges in every possible manner. The new municipal act provides that the person to administer justice in towns and cities must be a barrister of five years standing; and the local Courts, for the decision of local differences, have been taken away from those who administered them before, and supplied with barristers of five years standing! [Hear, hear.] The expenses of litigation were enormous. In England with 20 millions of inhabitants, they had 15 superior judges; in Canada, with 1½ millions, they had 20. Now, he would like to know if the public were prepared to submit to this incubus—this excrescence of the body politic, that seems to have got so firm a grip that, like the leech, it will never let go its hold till it is gorged with the life blood of its fainting victum. [Cheers.] He would propose those legal reforms which had been adopted in the State of New York, to simplify the pleadings in the first place; do away with the whole system of legal fiction, the John Does and Richard Roes; he would sweep them away at once. [Cheers and laughter.] He would have the pleadings in the language of common sense, so that any man of common sense should understand them. The plaintiff should set forth his case, the defendant reply, and the plaintiff make his rejoinder, in the language of common sense. Then with regard to indictments, they should be

drawn up in the language of common sense, so that the unfortunate criminal and the men of common understanding who are to pronounce his guilt or acquittal might be able to understand whereof he is accused. Mr. Gamble then produced a blue-book, which he styled a museum of curiosities, and read a tremendous list of salaries, and sums of money paid annually to lawyers, beginning with £1,666 13s. 4d. to Chief Justice Robinson, who, he remarked, was the man to be paid if any one was; he was an ornament to his country, as well as to his profession, and his name was associated with all that is brightest and purest: there also he found £600 for Mr. Killaly's travelling expenses, and £1500 to Mr. George Brown for the Penitentiary commission—an instalment, he supposed, on account; these commissions, he understood, were wonderfully increased in number, and used as a means of rewarding political friends, and that the amount of money expended in this way was very great. For his part, being desirous of ascertaining the truth of these allegations, he had lately, when in Montreal, applied for information to a party there, who appeared to be in the government secrets; that party was *Punch;* having expressed his desire to the old gentleman to be informed in the matter of these commissions, he kindly raised a curtain with his stick —the same stick with which he tilted the thimble and discovered the pea under Montreal—exposing to his view the thimble-riggers in deep conclave, trying to classify the disbursements for these same commissions in the public accounts, so as to fit them for the public eye, and over their heads was written—

Then Frank said to Bob, we are blown, my dear nigger,
We at last are found out to be loose in the figure,
We've sacked it, and spent it, and cannot repay,
Let us blow out our brains in a gemman like way.
[Great laughter.]

But to have done with this badinage, and return to that which was serious, too serious indeed to be laughed at. He must next allude to the Constitution of the country itself. Supposing he should ask any of his friends there, where that Constitution is? His legal friends surely know it is a matter for antiquarian research. He believed it was contained in five different Acts of Parliament, each act amending and repealing parts of the other acts; he believed parts of it were to be found in the Ordinances passed by the Council appointed under the 14th George III., the Ordinances of the Special Council and elsewhere for any thing he knew. For his part, he desired to have the Constitution written, and plain, so that the people of the country might know their rights as secured to them by the Constitution, and be able to point to it when necessary; he did not wish to see it so hid in a mass of rubbish that they cannot find out what rights are secured to them, without going to the legal gentlemen; he wanted it to be made plain and simple, so that those who run may read. He should be told, no doubt, this was downright Republicanism, but he contended it was downright Anglo-Saxonism. Go to the very foundation of the thing—the Municipal Act alluded to. Where did that come from? The gentleman who drew it up derived it, in all probability, from the laws of Massachussetts, and partially engrafted on it the law of New York—whence did the people of Massachusetts derive that system, doubtless they brought it with them from England. This very municipal system is Anglo-Saxon. In former times the parish affairs in England were managed by the select vestry, and the select vestry was elected by the congregation, then the whole people of the parish, and he believed to this day, the term select-men was retained in the New England States— indicating plainly its origin. England itself, has been styled a nest of little republics, one small republic within the other ; look at the voluntary associations for railroads, canals, and innumerable other purposes beyond the reach of individual exertion, are they not based upon the very principle of election which he was advocating. In Banking alone, were such associations cumbered with restrictive regulations, and he believed it would be well for England, and well for all those connected with her commerce, if these regulations were abolished. Then with regard to the outer case, or covering of these associations, the empire itself, what was it ? At the time when Her Majesty ascended the throne, she was only 18 years of age, and a girl 18 years of age nominally swayed the destinies of a hundred millions of people. He said nominally, for what does the thing itself prove ? but that the real power rested somewhere else ; that it in truth rested in the House of Commons—the representatives of the people, and that the power of the realm was exercised by those whom the people's representatives willed should exercise it. Gentlemen would see from this, that there was nothing contrary to the spirit of the British constitution in the plan he proposed, and that it was one which could be carried out in connection with Great Britain. Mr. Gamble concluded, by declaring his conviction that Great Britain would desire to maintain her position on this continent, and never would consent to annexation The whole commercial marine of the world, is 10,000,000 tons, of which 4,000,000 belong to Great Britain, and 3,000,000 to the United States, the other 3,000,000 are owned by the various other nations of the world ; now of the 4,000,000 tons that Great Britain owns. 500,000 are British North American; annexation would at once place the commercial marines of England and the United States on an equal footing, and for that reason alone, he did not believe England would, willingly, consent to annexation, though, at the same time it was his conviction that Great Britain was not prepared to go to war, either on that question, or on account of the Mosquito King ; the advocates for annexation need not fear Canada being made a battle field for British and American armies, the interest of both countries forbids collision. The consumption of cotton in Great Britain in 1849, is estimated at 2,000,000 of bales ; four-fifths of this came from the United States, from this cotton alone was derived 26 tof her 55 millions of exports, and the supply of this material has to Great Britain become a matter of national interest, second only to that of food for her myriads.

Mr. DIXON wished Mr. Gamble to explain how he intended to carry out the latter part of his resolution.

Mr. GAMBLE proposed to apply to the Legislature to sanction a Convention to amend the Constitution.

Mr. DIXON not being satisfied with this explanation, moved an amendment, to strike out all the original motion after the words " with our sister Provinces," and insert instead,

" To this end it is expedient for this Convention to lay down the principles of a Constitution for the said Union, and submit it to the people of Canada, and the other British Provinces, and through their representatives to the Imperial Government for confirmation."

Mr. E. G. O'BRIEN briefly seconded the amendment.

Mr. P. M. VANKOUGHNET after a short personal explanation relative to what took place on the preceding evening, addressed the Convention as follows :—The question before the Convention was whether or not it is expedient to obtain the authority of the Legislature for holding a General Convention of Delegates for the purpose of considering and proposing a new Constitution. The first part of the resolution setting forth the remedies needed, viz., protection, retrenchment, and a union of the Provinces, he cordially approved of, but he objected to the latter part of the resolution giving the means by which these remedies are to be obtained. He objected to it for this reason, because it would be utterly impossible for the Legislature to grant what was asked. The Legislature of this Colony is not a Legislature like that of England or the United States. The Legislature of this Province emanates from Great Britain; they derive their power from Great Britain ; they are in existence under the Union Act, which gives them certain powers and prescribes and limits them according to the terms of the act ; the Legislature have no power under that act of union to confer any portion of their power on the delegates of the people. He therefore objected to asking the Legislature for anything they could not do, it was mere child's play. The Legislature have no power whatever to grant the prayer of the petition, and it would be very absurd therefore for the Convention to declare by a resolution that it was expedient to go to the Legislature to ask what the resolution proposed, it would be a useless visit to the Legislature. This was his chief objection to the resolution. The Legislature cannot confer any power to alter the Constitution of the country, because they cannot alter the Constitution themselves; they may make any law they please under the Constitution, for giving it an effective working, but they cannot alter the Constitution, and if they cannot alter the Constitution, how can they delegate to others the power to do it ? He might be told " we admit all that, but all that we want the Legislature to do is to make our meetings legal—to give us the sanction of their authority, in order that obtaining that sanction we may go to the people with a semblance of authority that must command greater respect and interest." If that be the view of the supporters of the resolution it amounts to nothing. We have already the right to do what we are doing, we have a right to assemble together, and to call the people of the country together, and to propose to them any change in the Constitution, and endeavour so to influence the public mind as to secure the return to the Legislature of those who coincide in our views and opinions, but it is not to the Legislature that we must go to make the changes desired. He admitted that through the Legislature would be the most effectual way of obtaining the sanction of England to any changes in our Constitution, but the way to influence the Legislature is so to work on the public mind as to send men to Parliament to urge our opinions, this was the true course. Then supposing we have men in the Legislature who adopt the views that we send forth to the country, what can they do? They cannot adopt these great changes, they can only do to the people of England what we can do to the people of Canada; they must recommend England to make the change, unless indeed they are prepared to pass a vote to leave England altogether, and take the authority into their own hands. All the Legislature has the power to do is to pass a resolution recommending England to carry out our views; how absurd then to go to the Legislature to ask for a power, which, however well disposed they may be, they cannot confer. Mr. Dixon's resolution proposes, that instead of going to the Legislature they should go to the people; with that he (Mr. V.) agreed; but to go to the people having prepared a scheme of union, with that he at present disagreed. Eventually they would have to go to the country with a scheme of union, but the Convention was not prepared at present to draw up such a scheme. At the last Convention it was admitted on all hands that they were not sufficiently possessed of the condition, resources, history, and feelings of the people of the Lower Provinces, to enable them at once to adopt a scheme of union, or even to declare in favour of such a union; he would ask the Convention how much better were they off in this respect now than they were at Kingston? Had they any more information to enable them to decide the question better? He would only say for one, that anxious as he was for a union of the Provinces, he had been unable to obtain such information as would enable him to form a conclusive opinion upon the subject, much less to draw up a scheme of union with which to go to the people. For this reason, he thought Mr. Dixon's proposal premature, and would submit an amendment. He objected then to Mr. Dixon's resolution, because it was impracticable; no man in the Convention could be prepared to draw up a scheme of union without knowing something of the condition and resources of the other Provinces, and ascertaining something of their feeling respecting the proposed union. He might be told in reply, that their last arrangements for obtaining this information had ended in nothing. He admitted it—but were they to abandon their search for information, because the means they had already taken had resulted in nothing? It was useless for the Convention

to declare that a union was desirable, unless they could first ascertain that the other Provinces would agree upon details; they should consult the people of the Lower Provinces on the matter, instead of going to them with a scheme of union ready prepared. No man could regret the delay more than he did; but a matter like this, of more importance than anything which has occurred upon this Continent since the American Revolution, cannot be settled in a minute; the establishment of a new nation on the face of the earth, as these Provinces would be, if united, cannot be settled immediately. It was better to wait for weeks, for months, aye for years, than, by being too precipitate, to throw things into confusion, from which it would be difficult to relieve them. It was no argument to say that the country is labouring under great and growing evils, and that we must have a change, unless they were prepared to propose a change that would be really productive of good. It was in that spirit that he opposed a change which it had not been satisfactorily proved would benefit the country; not because he was one of those to whom Mr. Gamble had referred, who hold inviolate, constitutional rights, and assert the divine power of kings. He did not believe in the divine power of kings, but he did believe in leaving things as they are, until you have found out something that will improve them. He did not make these remarks to censure any of the changes proposed by Mr. Gamble; not because he objected to an elective Governor, and an elective Legislative Council; he should express his opinion on these points when the subject came up; it was not because he objected to any change, but because he had sufficient prudence and caution to ascertain if the changes proposed were going to benefit the country. He opposed the original resolution, because it was useless to appeal to the Legislature for a power which they could not grant, and he opposed Mr. Dixon's amendment as being premature, as he did not think they were in a position to draw up a scheme of union with which to go before the country.

Mr. GAMBLE was astonished at the arguments used by the last speaker. Was he to be told that it was not in the power of the representatives of the people of this country to appoint delegates to meet to consult about this matter with delegates from the other Provinces, and draft a constitution to be submitted to the people, and to make application to the people of England? Did not the Legislature every day delegate their power to others, by appointing commissioners for different purposes to carry out their objects, and why should they not do it in this case. He had no desire to bring on the matter improperly, but the amendment would cause too much delay. If they delayed long it would be impossible to keep this country a dependency of the British crown—there might be no British Provinces to unite. (Loud cries of hear, hear.)

Mr. VANKOUGHNET did not think the explanation relieved the difficulty. No one denied the right of the Legislature to appoint delegates to meet delegates from the other Provinces to consult about this matter, but the resolution was not to request them to appoint delegates from their own body, but to give the people the authority to appoint delegates. (Cries of spoke, spoke.)

Mr. READ supported the amendment; he disapproved of any important changes in the Constitution; the present Constitution was sufficient, if fairly carried out.

Mr. WILSON (Quebec) rose, in consequence of the censure cast by Mr. Vankoughnet on the committee appointed at the last Convention to meet the delegates from New Brunswick. (Mr. Vankoughnet denied he had censured them, he merely said they had done nothing.) That was the highest censure that could be cast on them; he maintained that they had done all that it was possible for them to do. Owing to some unfortunate circumstance, the publication of the reports of the proceedings of the last Convention was considerably delayed, but they were forwarded to the Lower Province as soon as possible But only one Province out of the four (New Brunswick,) sent delegates, and those gentlemen (Messrs. Robertson and Simmonds) were armed with no power whatever, except to confer with and ascertain the views of the League, and then to report them to the Association of New Brunswick. Under these circumstances, he apprehended that they could not have done more than they did. Their worthy Chairman had transmitted copies of the report to friends in Nova Scotia, and requested them to co-operate, but they had not done so, and he doubted much if the Nova Scotians cared anything about the matter. He approved exceedingly of Mr. Dixon's resolutions, for this reason, because the gentlemen from New Brunswick had told him that the Lower Provinces were looking to the Convention to lead them in the matter, and expected the League to devise a plan for the Union of the Provinces, so that by pursuing the caution of his learned friend, Mr. Vankoughnet, they would do nothing. He thought his learned friend was too cautious. What matters it whether the other Provinces are rich or poor and impoverished. We must take them for better for worse; the gentlemen from New Brunswick were alarmed at the amount of our public debt, but when they ascertained the extent of our public works, they said it was of no consequence.

Mr. JOHN DUGGAN disagreed entirely with Mr. Vankoughnet as to the power of the Legislature to appoint these delegates; it had been done again and again, it had been done in every commission appointed; a commissioner was the same as a delegate. He thought Mr. Gamble's resolution was very properly and carefully worded; it did not say for the purpose of drafting a constitution to be afterwards *adopted*, but *submitted*. He regretted the dictatorial style adopted by Mr. Vankoughnet in expressing his opinion, it was not calculated to promote harmony or goodwill in the Convention. He firmly believed that

there was not another professional gentleman in the room but Mr. Vankoughnet, who would deny that it was entirely within the scope of the Legislature to grant what was asked in this resolution. There was nothing illegal or unconstitutional in it; the power was exercised again and again, in the appointment of commissioners, which are the same as delegates. He (Mr. Duggan) would support Mr. Dixon's resolution, because it would bring them nearer to the point than Mr. Gamble's. At the Kingston Convention he had the honour to move a resolution to the effect that a union of the British North American Provinces would conduce to the prosperity of the Colonies and the integrity of the British Empire; on that occasion he told the Convention that if they did not adopt some measure of this kind and press forward with some remedy for the difficulty into which the Province was hastening, that at their door and at their door alone would lie the blame. Had the Convention adopted the course he then pursued, he asked them would the question of Annexation have been ever mooted in Montreal? He believed it would not; they would have shown the people a clear and tangible mode to get out of the difficulties by which they were surrounded, and given them something that would have engrossed their attention, but the Convention would not follow the course he proposed, they adopted a more cautious resolution, not thinking that the Province was on the very verge of a revolution and had it not turned out so? And now forsooth when the question of a dismemberment of the empire had actually come up—when a revolution was contemplated in the colony, Mr. Vankoughnet got up and asked for further delay, and to send delegates to Halifax at this season of the year, and have them to return to the constituencies that sent them, having done nothing to avert the threatened danger. For what had they met but to adopt a remedy for the condition of the country and prevent the dismemberment of the British empire? It was for no other object but this that he had come to the Convention; the dismemberment of the empire is at this moment going on, and perhaps before the time needed for Mr. Vankoughnet's delegates to return from Halifax had gone by, there might be no British Provinces to consult on the subject. (Cheers.) He did not think Mr. Vankoughnet was justified or borne out by facts in the censure he cast upon the Committee appointed by the last Convention; they communicated with the other Provinces but without success, for only two gentlemen from one of those Provinces attended, and they were without the power to consent or assent to anything. Under these circumstances he thought the Committee had done all that could be expected from them. He thought that by adopting Mr. Dixon's amendment they would be taking a very important step towards the accomplishment of the scheme of union.

Mr. GOWAN did not rise for the purpose of prolonging the discussion, for he concurred in every word which had fallen from the learned gentleman who had spoken last. He cautioned those of his friends in the Convention, who were like himself attached to British connection, to mark well the ground on which they stood. Each arrival proved that the ground was melting from under the feet of those who were attached to the British flag ; it was only this morning that he learnt that two Hon. members of the Legislative Council of the Province had come out in favour of annexation—(loud cries of name, name)—he hoped he was not to be called upon to name them—(no,no)—they were names which had hitherto commanded the respect and attention of every gentleman in the Convention; they were men, one of them largely engaged in the commerce and trade of the country, and the other had also a large stake in the country ; and these were men who, a few short months ago, would rather have been deprived of a limb than entertain the question of annexation, or separation from Great Britain. (Loud cries of hear, hear) Those, therefore, who were friends of the British flag had no time for delay, the question must be met, and met in a proper spirit. He could not agree in Mr. Vankoughnet's views. True, the Convention had the power to adopt a constitution, and send it forth to the public like a circular, or any other document, but it would fall lifeless and still-born on the people and Parliament of England, if not on the people and Legislature of this Province ; if you wish to reach England you must reach it through the constitution of the country. You can only influence the Government and Parliament of England through the Parliament of Canada ; any document they might adopt must be sent home by delegates ; if they sent home respectful petitions only, Lord Grey would put them under his feet, as he did the petitions of hundreds of thousands of his fellow subjects on a recent occasion—(loud cries of hear, hear)—if they would move the British Government they must do it through the Legislature of this country. Mr. Vankoughnet stated that the Legislature had not the power to grant what was contemplated by Mr. Gamble's resolution ; he (Mr. Gowan) contended that they had the power. This city has been given a constitution for its municipal government, and did his learned friend mean to say that the Corporation of this city does not possess the power to pass a by-law for the inhabitants of the city of Toronto to assemble in the different wards, and choose delegates, or commissioners, for the purpose of saying if the constitution in the act of Parliament is that suited to the interests of this city, or not, and having agreed on the form of government they think best, to submit it to the Parliament of the Province for ratification ? The same authority exists in the Legislature of this country to say that the people shall assemble when and where they please, under the authority of an Act of Parliament, to say what alterations they require in the constitution, and afterwards to be sent home to the Metropolitan Government as the form of Government the people of Canada think the best for their own interests. (Hear, hear.) If they wish to bring about any change in the form of Government

that was the only mode in which they could effect it. If the matter be delayed much longer friend after friend will fall away from our standard, and by-and-by but few will be found to rally round the old flag. (Loud cheers.) If they desired to carry out their views they must act promptly, or they would fail ; he cared not whether the Legislature answered to their call or not; if it did then their object was gained, if not the people of Canada would not fail to lay the responsibility on those who administered the Government of the Province, and refused to grant the demands of the people. (Cheers.) England professes to have given us self-government, we meet her on her own professions, and ask her for nothing further than she professes already to have given us ; if she has given us self-government, let it not be under the constitution which she has dictated to us, but under the constitution which we approve of. (Cheers.) He conceived that the suggestion contained in Mr. Gamble's resolution was the one the Convention ought to adopt, and he should therefore vote for it.

Mr. R. McDonald had been convinced by the arguments he had heard of the danger of further delay, and he should therefore vote for Mr. Dixon's amendment.

Mr. Aikman also supported the amendment, and on a different ground from any body else, viz: that it would give them something tangible with which to go before the country.

The President (Hon. George Moffatt,) here left the chair and addressed the Convention. The great plea urged in favour of the amendment is saving of time; now if that be the sole object, saving of time will equally be effected by adopting the resolution as it stands, and afterwards proposing the amendment as a subsequent resolution, to be submitted to the people. The great object is to save time; if we do not apply to the Legislature to further this object of a union of the provinces immediately, valuable time will be lost. If you adopted these resolutions, you would appeal to the people to call on the Governor General to dissolve the present assembly and call a new one ; if you are of opinion that the views you entertain are shared in by the people at large, the people will be with you, and you will obtain a dissolution of the Legislature, the same influences will enable you to send to the provincial legislature men who will carry out your views with respect to the union ; if you do not represent the feelings of the people of the country, all that you can propose here will be of no avail whatever, and all that you can do is to explain to the country, what in your opinion ought to be done, and leave it with the people of the country to decide on it, and move in it if they are of opinion that it is advisable to do so; if not, they will not move in it, and all you can do will not induce them to do it : all our labours are lost if the people are not with us. I have been told that the people are not prepared—that they want to understand our views ; I understand that we were sent here by the people, who said they were labouring under grievances and want redress;

they do not send us here to consult about the evils, but to find out the best means of obtaining redress: well, the resolutions of Mr. Gamble, in my opinion, point out the means of doing it. They first point out the state of the country—they then propose that a dissolution of Parliament should be asked for, and men sent to the Legislature to carry out the remedies we propose, viz, protection to native industry, retrenchment of the public expenditure, and a union of the Provinces: 'I am told now that it is necessary to delay to draft a constitution, to lay down the principles of the union, and lay them before the people, before you call upon the Legislature to act upon them. My view of the matter is, that if the Parliament was dissolved, and men were sent there who entertained the views that you entertain, they would proceed instanter to take the necessary steps to carry it out. We are told that the Legislature have not the power to carry out the suggestion contained in this resolution, but that has been very well answered—delegates are the same as commissioners. The Legislature have the power to adopt a resolution to propose to the other colonies a union of the Provinces, they then appoint commissioners to proceed to see if the other colonies will concur with them, and give them power to consider the matter, and propose to the several Legislatures, the principles on which it should be carried out; if the Legislature would take the initiative in the matter, they would bring it to a conclusion in much less time than in my opinion can be done by any other means. Time will therefore be gained by applying at once to the Legislature, and if you are of opinion that the present Legislature will not entertain the project you want, appeal to the country, to put forth petitions calling on the Governor to dissolve Parliament; if you carry the country with you, your opinions will be reflected in the Legislature, and you will be enabled to carry out the views you entertain, and which in my humble judgment are those best calculated to provide a remedy for the evils now abroad; nothing will be sufficient but that to prevent Annexation to the United States. Those who entertain the opinion that nothing but Annexation will prove an adequate remedy for our grievances, and charge the Convention with having done nothing, will unite with you in calling on the executive authority to exercise the royal prerogative in dissolving the House of Assembly, because they will by that means have an opportunity of sending to Parliament, men who will advocate their views. Those who look upon Annexation as a *dernier resort* will have the same chance; if they have not confidence in the men now returned to the Legislature, they will unite with you in calling on the Governor General to give the people of the country an opportunity of sending to Parliament fresh men under present circumstances to say what are their interests and wishes. I think this is the most favourable time in every point of view to call

on the Governor to exercise that prerogative. I think we shall gain by adopting the 3rd resolution, proposed by Mr. Gamble; it does not at all militate against our adopting a subsequent resolution, setting forth the principles on which the proposed union shall take place, but in my judgment it would have been sufficient if the subject had been argued broadly, as Mr. Gamble argued it. I think we should lose time if, without authorizing any appeal to the Legislature, we should adopt Mr. Dixon's amendment. (Hear, hear.)

After a few words from Mr. D'Arcy Boulton, Mr. Dixon's amendment was carried.

Mr. GAMBLE—It is now for the gentleman who moved the amendment to carry it out, that's all I can say.

Mr. DIXON gave notice that he would the first thing on Monday morning submit to the Convention the principles on which the proposed union should be carried out.

UNION OF THE PROVINCES.

The Report of the Committee of Conference, held at Montreal by Delegates from Canada and New Brunswick, was then taken into consideration in Committee of the Whole.—Mr. Aikman in the chair. [This report was published at length in the printed proceedings.]

Mr. WILSON (Quebec) rose and said, on the motion now before the Committee, I have prepared in the course of the morning four resolutions which I intend to submit to the consideration of the Convention. I am not ignorant of the important consequences that may follow the adoption of the resolutions I am about to propose. I am aware that they will involve consequences most serious in their result to this and the other colonies, if they are carried out. I am aware also that I shall be opposed probably in some of them by the talent of my learned friend, Mr. Vankoughnet, but I am prepared to take the responsibility. Much has been said about our connection with Great Britain, our love of monarchical institutions, our hatred of republicanism, and our detestation of democracy. When I look at a form of government and am led to admire it, I admire it in consequence of its adaptation to the people who support it. While a monarchical form of Government suits the people of England, I maintain that monarchy can never take root on this continent. I maintain that we are by nature, in our feelings and sentiments, attached to a free, and if you choose to call it so, a republican form of government. (Great cheering and cries of no, never.) Gentlemen may tell me never, but I can tell them that this sentiment does not entrench in the smallest degree on my loyalty and attachment to the British Empire. That very form of government which I now seek to induce the people of this colony to adopt, it is not the first time it has been adopted in the British possessions. At the time of the American revolution the State of Rhode Island, then, a colony of the British Empire, possessed the very form of government which I seek to establish when I ask the Convention to adopt these resolutions. Gentlemen talk about our present form of government, and say it is a transcript of the British form of government. I deny it, I say that we at present live under the government of a party, and that that party has the power to make the Legislative Council and Governor General do whatever they think fit; the two higher branches of the government, as they exist at present, are not independent, or a faithful representation of the Sovereign and the House of Lords.

[The speaker was here called to order by Mr. Hamilton, and a discussion ensued as to the way in which the business should be conducted, ultimately the report of the Committee of Conference was read and adopted, and the President having resumed his seat.]

Mr. WILSON renewed his address to the Convention. He said—I stated, when I was about to address you before, that forms of government, whatever they may be, are only good and to be admired so far as they are suited to the capacity and intelligence of the people. For instance, I believe that the form of Government which now exists in Russia—the Government of the Autocrat—is best suited to the people, and that if they had a form of government like that of the Americans they would not appreciate it, and the worst consequences would follow its adoption. I believe that the monarchical form of government is best suited to the people of England, that they would not understand the form of government which our neighbours enjoy south of line 45, but I believe also that the government they have south of line 45 is, in all its arrangements, best calculated for the inhabitants of the British Possessions on this Continent. I sincerely believe it to be the case, and I judge from the opinions of the people with whom I have associated. We have been told by some that we have in this Colony a transcript of the British Constitution. I deny it most positively. The Sovereign of England is an independent branch of that Government, she has the power to reject any bill if she disapproves of it, and if she should reject it the people of England would support her in the exercise of that power. The House of Lords is independent; they exercise a deliberative power over every measure brought before them. The House of Commons is independent, and they exercise the same power and deliberate upon all measures; but I would ask the gentlemen of this convention, if we have three independent branches of the government in this colony, exercising the same deliberative functions that they have in England? I say we have not, and that under the present mode of constituting the Government of this colony, we cannot have it. (Hear, hear.) To support anything like monarchy on this continent, you must have an aristocracy,—men of independence and intelligence, capable of retiring from the fatigues of business and the labours of life, and who have a large stake in the country, and it is no less the duty of these persons to stand by the liberties of the people than to protect the prerogative of the Crown. But what is our present constitution? We have an individual nominated to this Government professedly by the Sovereign but ostensibly and virtually by the Colonial Minister. Now it is within the range of possibility that some gentleman residing in this colony,—my friend Mr. Vankoughnet, for instance, might find it necessary to go to England, his professional ability and talent would bring him into notice, and he might become a member of the Government, be made Colonial Secretary, and Mr. Vankoughnet would in fact, send us a Governor-General! (Hear, hear.) I ask you, if that was to be the case, should we be satisfied with it? Is it right that an individual exercising one-third of the power of this government should be appointed by the gentleman who temporarily occupies Downing-street? (Hear, hear?) Then with regard to the appointment of the Legislative Council.— When the gentlemen now in power came into office, they found that that council did not suit them, they feared that there was a majority of the members differing from them, and the consequence was, that immediate application was made to England, and blank writs of mandamus sent out here; they were sent to Lord Elgin, not knowing whether the parties would accept or not; they came for the purpose of forming a Legislative Council of the political party now in power. (Hear, hear.)— Now I contend that we have not at present, three independent and separate branches of the Government. The two upper branches are simply, the first to record the proceedings of the House of Assembly, and the second, the instrument of the persons in power. (Hear, hear.) In order that we may have what is really and truly the spirit of the British Constitution, a government of checks—in order that we may have a Governor clothed with authority, and an independent Legislative Council, I maintain that these officers should be elected by the people, (Cheers,) because when they hold the power they possess from the people of this Colony, those powers will be respected, whereas at present they are not. (Hear, hear.) I will go further, and state in what manner I would suggest that the Legislative Council and Governor should be elected. I mentioned this subject to the gentlemen from New Brunswick, and it was freely discussed; they said they did not think the people of New Brunswick would object to it,—but that one thing they would stipulate for was, that they should be represented in the Legislative Council by the same number of representatives as the people of Canada, on the same principle as the Senate of the United States. Well, I would require that the parties electing the members of the Legislative Council should have a property qualification, and also, that the party sitting in the Legislative Council should have a property qualification. I would also arrange that it should be divided into eight separate portions, and that an eighth portion should retire every year, so that you could never change suddenly the character of the House; it would be virtually and in fact a much more conservative body than we have at present. I would then suggest, for the nomination of the Governor General, that a certain number of members should be appointed by the Lower House, corresponding to the number of members in the Upper House, and that these two bodies should name the individual whom they thought proper to be the Governor. I believe that under an arrangement of that kind, we should have a much more conservative constitution than we have at present. The present constitution is one of the worst possible kinds of democracy: parties are fighting for office, and as soon as they get in, they have to turn their opponents out, and put their friends in, to plunder the public for a time: so that we are continually plundered by one party or the other. (Cheers.) I also believe that the Government of this Colony should have the power to legislate for the interests of the inhabitants on all matters connected with their commercial or civil interests, without the intervention of the authority of Great Britain. (Cheers) It is most likely that many gentlemen here w say, Why, you are going for independence. I am only going to assume that position which the British press and Government have distinctly told the colonists they must take,—that is, that we can manage our own affairs. But, how can the Government tell us that they will leave us to the management of our own affairs and at the same time appoint two out of the three branches of the Government of the country? (Cheers.) They practically give the lie to their professions, as was lately shown in the repeal of the incorporation of Bytown, which did not involve either the honour of the crown or the integrity of the Empire. No doubt rests upon my mind, that a time will come, when the British Provinces must take a position of their own. I hope, gentlemen, that that time is distant. I hope never to see the day when I shall cease to live under the flag of old England, and I believe that the course I am now pursuing is the only course that can preserve these colonies as a portion of the empire. (Loud cries of hear, hear.) Sir, because I ask her Majesty to grant to these colonies the right of naming their own Governor and Legislative Council, will these concessions entrench on my feelings of loyalty? —make me love my Sovereign less, or feel less devotion to her service? I say not, on the contrary, it will rivet me more closely to her. I shall see that the Government of England has acted like an indulgent parent, and trusted me with the management of my own affairs, as soon as I am able. (Hear, hear.) I do contend, that with the exception of Lords Sydenham and Metcalfe, we could have found infinitely better men than the Governors we have had for twenty years past. (Loud cheers)— Why, then, should Great Britain deny us these things? I believe she will not deny it. (Hear, hear.) I believe that if application is made she will grant it. (Cheers) Many of my friends, who are advocates of annexation, have told me, "oh Mr. Wilson, you are just doing what we want." I do believe, that if I were an annexationist, I would take the very course I am taking, but I want to bring those gentlemen with me, to obtain that constitution for these colonies which I seek; and if they do not find

that constitution better than annexation, then I'll go with them for annexation. (Cheers.). I have not the slightest hesitation in saying, that that government is best which will best suit the interests, welfare, and prosperity of the people. Sir, I believe that we can place ourselves in a position to remain in connexion with Great Britain, infinitely superior to anything we can get from a foreign power. Those gentlemen who are in favour of Annexation to the United States, cry out, oh, you will never do good till you are annexed, but there is not one who has come forward, and said on what conditions we are to go into the union. Now, I say, that if we are to go into the union on the same conditions as the other States, they are conditions that I would reject as most destructive of our interests; we are told, that if we become part of the States, we shall have American capital and American industry, and protection to home industry, and I believe, whey I have stated that, that I have stated nearly all, but they forget to give us the other side of the picture; that we must yield to the United States the revenue derived from the importations into this Province, tax ourselves for the purpose of carrying on the Provincial Government, assume our share of the United States debt, and give up to the Central Government, the whole of the unappropriated lands of the colony. (Loud cries of hear, hear.) I don't blame gentlemen for advocating annexation, because I believe they wish it sincerely, but I look on this question, and the manner in which it is advocated, as involving in my judgment that which is criminal. (Hear, hear) Had I been an annexationist, I would not have taken the course that they have done, I would have represented my condition to England, and asked to have done so and so, and so and so, and if she had refused it, then I would be justified in taking their course; but when I read the Montreal Manifesto, it seems to me to contain one sentence which is humiliating to every Anglo-Saxon who puts his name to it. They say, we do not wish this annexation, provided England does not think it desirable; they first tell us that the country will be ruined unless we have annexation, and yet they say they don't think it desirable unless England will consent.— The thing is ridiculous, it is a position that no Englishman should assume. If I thought England could not redress the evils of which we have a right to complain, I have another course, and a course that many of my countrymen have taken before. I would first use every constitutional means to obtain my rights, but if they were still withheld from me, I would meet power by power, I would maintain my rights. (Loud cheers.) But Sir, I am satisfied, that even if the United States would consent to take us, that they never would be permitted by England to take one single acre of this country, so that as far as annexation goes, I am satisfied that it is unattainable and impracticable. (Cheers.). If every inhabitant of this colony was to call out for annexation to-morrow, and the citizens of the United States were ready to receive us,

Great Britain would say, we wont allow it, and it could not be done. It is said by some of my friends, oh, that is all nonsense, the United States could thrash Great Britain. If I had been a younger and better man, I would have put my fist in the face of him that said it. The United States go to war with Great Britain! Why there is not a more vulnerable power on earth than the United States, one more easily crippled; they have the most extensive commerce of any nation in the world, there is not a part of the globe where their vessels are not floating. What navy have they to protect that commerce, not only if they were to go to war with Great Britain, but with the most insignificant power in Europe; if that power had a navy at all, it would easily cripple the United States. But they have a more dangerous enemy still in the Southern population; there they have 3,500,000 bondsmen. Great Britain would only have to land an army, and give arms and ammunition to the Southern blacks, and they will raise up an army that our neighbours could not put down for centuries. (Cheers.) The United States will never go to war, nor will they take these colonies, or open any negociations, till the consent of England shall have been obtained. The whole question rests on the will of the Imperial Government. I will next proceed to notice the prospect which these colonies have, if united under an economical Government, with good laws. I have carefully looked over the resources of the British possessions on this continent, and if I had been asked to select a section of the globe, capable of sustaining a large population in wealth and abundance, I should have said, that place is the British North American provinces. (Cheers.) Mr. Gamble has alluded to the mineral wealth of Nova Scotia, I will go further, and notice her large capabilities for manufacturing, and her unrivalled supply of coal; you have every material for establishing manufactures to an unlimited extent, except the supply of labour, and the same may be said of New Brunswick and Lower Canada; and then I come to Western Canada, you have the finest agricultural country in the world, one better capable of producing wheat than any part of the United States; go further west you have the Mines of Lake Superior and Huron, possessing inexhaustible wealth; why if there be any country in which the people can be happy and prosperous, it is these Provinces. (Cheers.) Establish a good economical Government; establish laws giving protection to home industry, amend your banking and currency laws, and then you may bid defiance to competition, and instead of looking upon our Southern neighbours with envy, they will have to look to us and envy our prosperity; instead of our emigrating to them, they will immigrate to us, this Province will become the receptacle of the surplus wealth of Europe. (Cheers.) I hope and trust that this Convention will do something to satisfy the wishes of the people. I yield to no man in my desire to continue our connexion with Great Britain, but I am satisfied that the only possible way of preserving that connexion, is to lay before the British Go-

vernment what we want, and what I believe to be contained in the resolution I submit to this Convention, and I believe we shall obtain it, and have nothing to seek for, and having the strongest feelings of affection and loyalty to our Sovereign, shall take a pride in preserving the integrity of the empire. (Loud cheers.) He moved the first of his resolutions.

Resolved,—" That, whether protection or reciprocity shall be conceded or withheld, it is essential to the welfare of this colony and its future good government, that a Constitution should be framed, in unison with the wishes of the people, and suited to the growing importance and intelligence of the country, and that such Constitution should embrace a union of the British American Provinces, on mutually advantageous and fairly arranged terms, with the concession from the mother country of enlarged powers of self-government."

Mr. JOHN DUGGAN seconded the resolution, which was carried unanimously.

MR. WILSON then moved his 2nd resolution, which was seconded by Mr. Gowan.

Resolved,—" That under the altered commercial policy of Great Britain, by which the differential duties in favour of Colonial produce have been largely repealed, and the Agricultural and Commercial interests of British dependencies subjected to the severest competition in her markets with foreign rivals independent in their Legislative action, it is obviously unjust to perpetuate the Imperial power to interfere with the proceedings of the Colonial Government, adopted to foster and advance our social and industrial welfare."

Mr. E. G. O'BRIEN said, that the resolution appeared to him to have a tendency of a very startling nature; he thought Mr. Wilson was leading the Convention step by step a little further than they would any of them like to go—indeed, to absolute independence. (Cheers.) The effect of this resolution, if he understood it rightly, would be to prohibit the interference of the Imperial Government in our legislation.

Mr. WILSON explained, that we were still to remain in connection with Great Britain, and to pass no act that would endanger the integrity of the empire.

Mr. O'BRIEN was still afraid of the tendency of the resolution, and would like to know what was to follow it.

The remaining two resolutions were accordingly read by Mr. Wilson, proposing that the Governor and the Legislative Council should be elected, and not appointed by the Crown.

Mr. GOWAN contended, that the two last resolutions had no connection with the one now before them.

Mr. DIXON thought that the latter clause of the resolution evidently implied, in as positive language as it was possible to use, that it would be unjust for the Imperial Government to interfere at all with our legislation, where our industrial and commercial pursuits are concerned. Supposing some of these gentlemen who advocate annexation were to come forward and persuade the Legislature that it was absolutely necessary for the industrial and commercial interests of the Province that we should be annexed to the United States, would Great Britain have no right to interfere then? he considered that the language of the resolution was not congenial with the British Constitution, to say nothing of the two that were to follow.

Mr. GAMBLE could not see how any gentle man who had voted in favour of protection could object to this resolution. Did gentlemen desire that Downing Street should have the power to interfere with our industrial pursuits? If they did not, they must go for this resolution. (Loud cries of hear hear.)

Mr. O'BRIEN suggested, that as the resolutions involved organic changes of immense importance, they should be printed, so that members could know what they were voting for. (Cries of no no, and question.)

Col. FRASER would rather have the question taken at once; as a British subject he would never consent to pass this resolution, and as to the other two HE WOULD DIE FIRST. (Roars of laughter, and great cheering.)

Mr. O'BRIEN moved the postponement of the discussion until the resolutions could be printed.

Mr. WILSON---We could not pass laws giving protection to native industry but what they would be subject to be over-ruled by Great Britain.

Mr. VANKOUGHNET did not clearly understand the resolution, and would vote for nothing he did not understand; he was in favour of postponing the discussion.

Mr. FERRES thought that gentlemen, especially those residing in Toronto, should consider the convenience of the delegates from a distance, and not cause unnecessary delay.

The motion for postponement was then put and lost.

Mr. O'BRIEN objected to the tendency of the resolution; *ce n'est que le premier pas qui coute,* and here the first step was taken with a vengeance. He moved in amendment the following, seconded by Mr. DIXON:

That while it is our great ambition to build up in the British Provinces of North America, a British people, actuated by those high moral and religious principles, combined with that spirit of integrity and freedom which has raised Great Britain to the highest station among the nations of the world, it is also our duty both to create at home and to seek abroad a market for the products of our own industry. And if the supposed interests of Great Britain will not admit of protection to Colonial products in her market; and if she will not, or cannot open the markets of Foreign countries, and especially of the United States of America, for the admission of Colonial products and manufactures, we shall of necessity be driven by a continuation of the present policy of the Mother Country to seek the welfare of our own people irrespectively of her interests, or her influences.

The reading of the resolution was received with loud laughter, and on being put from the chair, after a word or two from the mover and seconder, was rejected.

Mr. BENJAMIN could not see why they should bring charges against the Home Government, without ascertaining their truth: he moved in amendment, seconded by Mr. MILLER:

That if the interests of the British people will not admit of protection to Colonial products in the markets of Great Britain, then will it become not merely the duty, but the inevitable necessity, of Colonists to create at home, or to seek abroad a market or markets for the products of their own industry; and thus by following the example of the Mother Country, seek the wishes of their own people, having inview not only their imme-

diate prosperity, but the future prospects of this our country. That in order to enable us to regulate these markets to our own advantage, and for our own safety it is necessary that we should obtain from Great Britain the control of the River and Gulf of St. Lawrence, and the power of imposing as we please, imposts upon British or Foreign goods, entering our markets.

Mr. GOWAN considered that it was mere quibbling or nibbling to ask only for the absolute controul of the Gulf and River St. Lawrence.—[Mr. BENJAMIN then altered the amendment, and made it "internal waters"] Some gentlemen had asked in what instances had Great Britain interfered? He would name some instances of interference on the part of Great Britain, which he trusted no gentleman in the Convention would tolerate. Did not Lord Grey, on the petition of a house in Glasgow, send a despatch to Lord Elgin, enclosing it, and saying that the tariff which had been passed by the Legislature of this country, and become the law of the land, had been assented to without his attention being called to it, and he wished to have the tariff altered to meet the views of the Glasgow house. (Hear, hear.) Was not that interference with the commercial interests of the Province? (Cheers.) He for one was prepared to say that the British Government should not have the right of interference in our own local and domestic affairs. Had not a citizen of this very city to go home, at the close of the last session of Parliament, to beg at the Colonial Office that the assent might be given to a bill for making a Railroad from this city to Lake Huron, because some persons said that the principle of a lottery was embraced in it; when a bill petitioned against by 100,000 inhabitants of this Province, involving a great principle, almost the question of allegiance to the Crown, could not be withheld, but the Royal assent must be given to it, in defiance to the wishes of the people, but a mere paltry Municipal Bill incorporating a town, or a railroad, must be kept back. He was not prepared to maintain a form of Government that admitted of these things. He desired to have an independent form of Government, and if we stand up for our rights we shall get them. (Cheers.)

At the suggestion of the Chairman, the word "absolute" was expunged.

Mr. MILLER seconded the amendment.

Mr. DUGGAN would vote for the original resolution, because he did not wish the prosperity of this Colony to hang on the notions of Sir Robert Peel, or any other British statesman

Mr. HATT also supported the resolution.

Mr. MACK said that fortunately for himself and the meeting, he could not occupy more than ten minutes, as they were to adjourn at six, but he had only a word to say upon this question, as remarks had been made in the course of the debate, on which he felt compelled to say a word or two. He thought the time had gone by for the people of this country to make use of the language of adulation towards the Imperial Government. He believed he was known to be utterly opposed to anything like annexation; but it was for the express purpose of seeing the connection continued and perpetuated that he should vote for Mr. Wilson's motion as it stood. He did not think there was any danger in making use of a threat at the present moment, provided it be one that the British Government and people feel that we can put into execution. It was useless to grumble or growl, and *promise* to do things which we never intend doing, and therefore he was prepared to vote for this resolution, and for others, which would, perhaps, be a little stronger than the annexationists could swallow. He saw nothing in this resolution but language that had frequently been used, that the interference must be one only of mutual liberty and forbearance. The day has come when the people of this Colony are perfectly competent to manage their own affairs; and if allowed to manage their own affairs, he could see no danger of a separation from the mother country. It was not the interference they complained of, so much as the inconsistency of it. The question was out whether the act was a just one, but whether Sir Robert Peel or Lord Grey should have office.— That was not the position for the pe ple of British America at the present day. We must, if we wish to be connected with England, have that sufficiency of self-government which will enable us to feel honestly that we are freemen, independent of any interference but that of which a parent may take in its children's affairs But the interference of a Government which may change its policy, and tamper with the affairs of this great Colony, cannot be endured. But he thought he saw a remedy for these evils in what has been done here to-day. The movement for annexation is helping us out of these evils. He (Mr. lack) disapproved of the annexation manifesto as much as any man, but he must confess that when he saw so many good men, and men wh se wisdom he revered, signing it, he could not but feel that if that document produced the same effect in England as it had done here, that it would turn the attention of England to us, and that was all that was needed. The English people have been, in regard to these Colonies, like the inhabitants of Laputa, in Dean Swift's novel, they are so philosophically indifferent to what is passing out of their own land, that nothing will wake them up but a slap on the cheek. (Cheers.) This resolution would show them that whilst one party look to annexation as the only remedy, the more moderate party think that self-government will be the best remedy, For these reasons he did not believe that England would refuse us anything we require in a loyal and right way.— (Cheers.)

The amendment was lost, and the original motion of Mr. Wilson was carried; after which the Convention adjourned till Monday.

MONDAY, Nov. 5, 11½ A. M.

The Convention sat for some time with their doors closed on Monday morning. When the Reporters were admitted—

Mr. Forsyth was on his legs, seconding Mr Wilson's resolution in favour of an elective Legislative Council. He had been contending that if we had had a body of men elected by the people. they would rather have trampled under their feet the commissions by which they were styled "Honourable," than have acted as the existing Legislative council did, with reference to the Rebellion Losses Bill; they would be men of a very different stamp and calibre from these,— men selected by the people from the wealth and intelligence of the country. The Resolution was as follows:

Moved by Mr. WILSON, seconded by Mr. FORSYTH, that it be

Resolved—That regarding the good of the people as the object of all Government, and recent events having proved to this Convention that the present mode of constituting the Legislative Council, is dangerous to its independence, and contemplating a Union of the British American Provinces, it is the opinion of this Convention that this branch of the Government should be elected.

Mr. DIXON moved the following amendment, viz. :—

That whereas, after mature deliberation and discussion, this Convention has recorded its solemn conviction, that the social, commercial, and political condition of the British North American Provinces, and more especially the Province of Canada is such, that a much longer continuance in their present state will lead to confusion and civil strife, and that the remedies best calculated to restore prosperity to their drooping interests are, a Union of the British North American Provinces, Protection to Native Industry, and a rigid Economy in the administration of their several Governments; and that in order to secure these great blessings with the least possible delay, it is highly necessary to call the attention of the people of Canada to the principles upon which it would be beneficial and safe to unite and consolidate the several interests of the said Provinces.

It is therefore Resolved—That the principles best adapted for securing these objects are—

First— The full enjoyment and exercise, by each Province, of all the social, religious and political freedom guaranteed to us by our present institutions, or as they may hereafter be amended, to promote our social comfort and happiness, by affording us the perfect control of all that is strictly local in our government, including our roads and canals (with the exception of the great thoroughfares open to the United Provinces,) together with our civil jurisprudence and industrial pursuits.

Second—By establishing a perfect equality in inter-Provincial rights—i the participation of equal trading and commercial privileges—the free and full use (upon terms of strict equality) of rivers, canals, and roads, together with an equal distribution of the public burthen and public revenue, in proportion to the consumption of each Province.

Third—By a perfect and untrammeled intercourse with each Province in carrying out the principle of free trade amongst ourselves as a united people.

Fourth—By consolidating our interests and wants in one general principle of legislation for the assistance, direction and control of our commerce, in such a way as to impress it with a national character, and preserve our industrial pursuits from a ruinous competition, and an unequal pressure upon each other,—by creating and sustaining a national credit and self-respect throughout the world,—by establishing one general code of criminal jurisprudence, a general and uniform currency, and a general bankrupt law,—by well regulated postal communications, and by a willingness to yield minor advantages for the general good.

Mr. GOWAN pointed out that the amendment and original m tion were not inconsistent with one-another: he objected to Mr. Dixon's motion being put as an amendment.

Mr. DIXON then addressed the Convention. He considered a remark made by Mr. Gamble on Saturday evening, very ungracious: when his (Mr. Dixon's) amendment was carried, Mr. Gamble said "Well, I leave it to the gentleman to carry it out." Now he (Mr. D.) had no desire to go into the matter, but when he was pushed into doing a thing, he did not choose to be beaten, and he had therefore hastily drawn up what he conceived to be the principles on which a union of the Provinces should be based, and he now submitted it to the Convention with the greatest deference, and was perfectly ready to assent to any improvement that might be suggested. He thought it essentially necessary that the Convention should submit some such scheme to the country. It was arranged at the Kingston Convention that the Central Committee should meet delegates from the Lower Provinces, and it was expected that the result of that conference would be something to submit to the country. Through causes which it was unnecessary he should go over, that plan had failed, and he considered that it was now the imperative duty of the Convention to draw up something to which to direct the attention of the people of the country. It was all very well to talk about submitting these things to the Legislature. How many things had been submitted to the Legislature? (Hear, hear.) He (Mr. Dixon) recollected signing an address to the Governor-General, and he alluded to him without any intention of derogating from the high position he occupies, but he was determined never again to associate himself with anything to be submitted to His Excellency the Governor General, because the petition he formerly signed had been kept in the back ground, along with the petitions of 100,000 others, which should have been laid before the Queen, and to which they had a right to a reply. (Loud cheers.) No, he would rather appeal to the people of this country and go before them with some good and substantial remedy for the grievances of which they complain. He would now briefly revert to the principle contained in the sketch of a constitution which he had prepared. It had long been a cause of public complaint that there was a want of controul in all our local matters in the constitution under which we live. In his opinion it was not so much a want of controul as a misdirection of the controul that there is—a want of something to put the controul of our public affairs in such a shape that we can put our hands on it and correct it if any thing goes wrong. Now the first part of his resolution embodied the principle on which this controul can be efficiently based; it not only guaranteed the liberty we now enjoy, but would extend that freedom and liberty On this point he would yield the palm to no man. He was a warm and zealous advocate of that liberty which he considered to be man's inalienable right, consistent with a proper controul and the general good of the country. These provinces are at present in such a position that it becomes essentially necessary that some steps should be taken to unite our interests. We are at present like so many little petty kingdoms or republics, without any efficient controul. There is no union of interests—no bond of cement—nothing calculated to unite us together in one common brotherhood for our united and individual welfare. The principle embodied in this amendment provided for such a general union of interests and a just participation in all the benefits and blessings which the country can possibly enjoy, and

he thought there was little or nothing in it but what every man could assent to. One argument he had heard urged by friends, and seen advanced in the public prints, that there never could be a union of interests. He differed from this opinion; he felt satisfied that such a union could be effected. It had been well and justly said, that it could not be expected—that England could not herself expect to hold this part of British North America for ever. (Hear, hear.)

A time for separation must come, and it is therefore expedient to prepare for it, and lay the ground-work of such a constitution, which will provide for the perpetuation of that which as Britons we hold dear. (Cheers.) He thought the amendment he held in his hand provided for this; he did not think that it in any way infringed on the rights of British subjects, and it provided for a general union of interests. He maintained that the individual interests of these British Provinces have grown to such a magnitude, and their trade so much increased, that it becomes absolutely necessary for every man to look for some project of uniting them for the general good; if they were not united, it was bu. natural to expect that these Provinces would one by one drop into the neighbouring union (Hear, hear.) By this union of the Province, it was proposed to consolidate their strength, "Union is strength." is an old maxim; and if we are to accomplish anything, it must be by united efforts. He (Mr Dixon) went a great way with Mr Gamble in his desire for protection to native industry, but he would not by that protection swamp the agricultural interests of the country. England affords at this moment an example of the evils of such a policy; in England, the manufacturing interest has risen to such a gigantic extent, that it is, in fact, swamping the rural pursuits, which have ever been the best blessing to the nation; he would like to see the two equally proportioned and protected. They had all long felt the necessity of a uniform Currency in these Provinces that too would be effected by the union proposed. Then, too, a general Bankrupt law was necessary for the protection of trade and commerce; the present Bankrupt law is a curse instead of a benefit to the community, and the only way in which this very desirable object could be obtained, would be by a union of the Provinces. A good and efficient postal arrangement was another much needed reform— for though we had been endeavouring to obtain the entire controul of the Post Office, resolution had followed resolution, and communication succeeded communication, but without producing any result. The next question to be decided was, what kind of union would be most beneficial and practicable. Some gentlemen supposed that our interests would be better consolidated by a Legislative Union and some features about a Legislative union certainly were desirable, but he was perfectly satisfied that the position in which we would be placed for many years is such, that a Legislative Union would never answer. We have seen enough of the evils of such a union, in the union between Upper and Lower Canada. In his opinion local legislatures would be best adapted to secure our local interests; by this means harmonious and good government would be secured. In order to effect this, he would not adopt Mr. Wilson's scheme of an elective Legislative Council, nor would he wish to see the evils exist which now exist, with regard to that body. He contended that there never had been a greater specimen of pure democracy manifested, than had been manifested in this country, by the packing of the Legislative Council. (Loud cheers.) The Legislative Council is made subservient to the party in power; it was a farce to call that the British Constitution, that equally and well balanced constitution, upon which we have so justly prided ourselves Such a state of things as this, he conceived to be directly contrary to the best interests of this country and of the Imperial Government. In order to effect a change in this respect, he would be in favour of having the Legislative Council elected by the several local assemblies, but as he was not willing that the local assemblies should have in their power to elect individuals hostile to British connection; he would give to the Imperial Government the power of vetoing any appointment which they might deem dangerous to the connection; he felt satisfied, that it would be only upon very grave and serious charges that such a power would be exercised. This was all he would ask Great Britain to concede, and he was satisfied that if she would concede what he had now proposed, she would grant us that which would tend to promote the general interests of these provinces, and the extension and perpetuation of her own domain.

After some debate on a point of order, Mr. Dixon withdrew his amendment, and substituting one in its place, declaring that the Legislative Council should be elected by the people, subject to the approval of the Crown.

Mr. GOWAN said the question before the Convention was, whether it was desirable that the Legislative Council should be elected by the people, or chosen by the Crown. He was in favour of an elective Legislative Council, because by referring to the unfortunate collisions and divisions which took place in the old Thirteen Colonies, now the United States of America. gentlemen would find this "great fact," that those colonies which possessed the freest institutions were the last to rebel, (great cheering); and the little colony of Rhode Island, which possessed the power of electing not only its Legislative Council, but its Governor, remained for some time, till it was forced on by the other colonies, before it would consent to rebel. (Cheers.) And being sincerely desirous to preserve our connexion with the Mother Country, he would look to the beacon that history holds up to our view, and when he found that the colonies that were not so free, were the first to plunge into rebellion, and that those that possessed elective institutions held out the longest, he would profit by the lesson, and being a faithful and attached subject to the Crown of Great Britain, he desired that our institutions should be sufficiently free to leave nothing in the

neighbouring Republic for us to envy. On this ground, he was in favour of elective institutions for this colony, and particularly for the election of the Legislative Council. He appealed to those gentlemen who were strongly attached to party, to support this principle, and on this ground; the highest officers we have at present the right of electing are our Municipal Corporations; and the Wardens of every District from here to the Eastern extremity of Canada West, are with one exception, Conservatives. This showed that if the elective principle were fully carried out, we should have a very different class of men in power from what we have at present. The amendment proposed that the great principle of an elective Legislative Council being conceded, it would be desirable to give the Crown a veto on the appointments. He was opposed to this amendment, as he felt confident it would be a source of constant irritation, the remedy would be worse than the disease. Lord Grey, or Lord Stanley, or whoever was Colonial Minister for the time being, could not possibly know anything of the qualifications of the gentlemen elected, he must be told it by some secret and irresponsible person unknown to us; it would destroy the principle of responsibility, and bring the Crown into direct collision with the people, and keep up the state of irritation which we at present complain of.— If we are to have the principle of an elective Legislative Council granted, we ought to have it free and unrestricted. (Cheers.)

Mr. ROLLAND MCDONALD would vote against both the original motion and the amendment. When the Municipal Council Act was first passed the Wardens of the Districts were appointed by the Crown, but under the alteration since made in the law, the Councils elect their own Wardens. The same remark applied to the District Treasurers, who, although formerly appointed by the Crown. are now appointed by the District Councils. The Clerks, too, were at first selected by the Governor, from a list of three, which was submitted by the Council of each District; each Council now elects its own Clerk. He (Mr. McD.) felt satisfied that, if the principle proposed by the amendment were applied to the Legislative Council. it would not work, for the first time a person elected by the people was rejected by the Crown. there would be a collision, and the same individual would most likely be re-elected. He was, therefore, opposed to the amendment. The Legislative Council must either be appointed by the Crown, or elected by the people. Then, as to the main question—shall we have an elective Upper House or not. It was well known to those who were at the Kingston Convention, that he (Mr. McD) was decidedly opposed to electing the Upper House; he was so still, he was sorry he could not change his opinion, but he was not so violently opposed to it now as then. And perhaps he would be better satisfied upon the whole if the Convention carried it against him (Cheers.) Still he would not compromise himself, he would record his dissent from the resolution, and reserve to himself the power of saying hereafter— "oh. it has turned out just as I expected, and I am not to blame." (Laughter.) He was not prejudiced one way or the other. He consider-ed that in the question of an elective Legislative Council was involved the question whether we are to have British institutions or American. It is singular that when we stick to British insti-tutions, we are, in point of fact, sticking to insti-tutions far more democratic than those of the United States. He would explain why. The House of Lords was placed there to check the encroachments of the people on the one side, and the Crown on the other; but though it may be so in theory, it has ceased to be so in prac-tice; the advance of liberty has been such as to throw the whole power of the people of Great Britain into the House of Commons, and if we desire to follow the British constitution we must follow that course here. He desired to carry out Responsible Government honestly. They might talk about the veto in England, but it has never been exercised since the revolution. The Queen of Great Britain has not one-tenth the power that the President of the United States has got. (Cheers.) He would admit that the American government is more conservative than ours. In England, the whole power is in the House of Commons; in Canada, the whole power is in the House of Assembly; and if the system of checks be put in, the responsibility of the administration is destroyed. This was the great difference be-tween the American and British institutions. How can you make the ministry responsible for their acts, if you have a Governor and Legisla-tive Council over whom they have no control? If you put in those checks, you must give up the idea of a responsible administration; the President must be everything, and the whole system must be changed; they must give up the idea of having a transcript of the British constitution. He was not prepared as yet to admit that the American institutions are better than ours, and he was not therefore prepared to go for an elective upper house. When they spoke of an elective Legislative Council, it was not meant, he supposed, to bring it into imme-diate operation, but only in the event of a union (Hear, hear, from Mr. Wilson) If it were pro-posed to establish it at once, he would go dead against it, because we have not the material—we are not prepared for it. In case of a federal union, the different Houses of Assembly would elect the upper house, but he took it for granted it was not considered advisable to do that now Would not the whole object be gained by limit-ing the number of councillors? His friend Mr. Wilson shook his head—he should therefore be compelled to vote against both the amendment and the resolution When the question of an elective Legislative Council was brought for-ward at the last Convention, he (Mr. McDon-ald) foretold that on a future occasion, when Mr. Wilson thought they were sufficiently enlight-ened, the question would be brought up again, along with that of an elective Governor, and his prophecy had come right. He was then op-posed to an elective Governor, and an elective upper house, and he felt satisfied that no man present could deny that if we had an elective

Governor, the same man would be Governor who is Governor now. (Loud cries of "no, no.") If there was an election at this moment, Mr. Lafontaine, who is Governor now, would be Governor. (Laughter, and cries of no, no.)—He would mention one thing to shew how in-consistent people are. Mr. Papineau rebelled for the purpose of getting an elective upper house, and they put down Mr. Papineau and the few rebels in Upper Canada, for asking for the very thing they were now themselves asking for. (Hear, hear.) Who would have foretold that after putting down Mr. Papineau in 1837, they would have been asking for the same thing in 1849. (Hear, hear.) Mr. Papineau's grand panacea for all the evils the country suffered under, was an elective Legislative Council, and now they (the Conservatives) were seeking the same thing! They were travelling altoge-ther too fast. Mr Gowan spoke of two parties, Conservatives and Reformers, but these were not the two parties now, it was quite a mistake to suppose so. The old parties are so cut up and divided that there are no such things as Reformers and Conservatives; the great ques-tion now is annexation, or anti-annexation.— (Cheers, and cries of question.) When he joined the League one of the things he promis-ed himself was, to assist in ousting the pre-sent ministry, because he conceived they were not acting for the advantage of the country; but that question had now become merged in a larger question. That was a ques-tion which, like the rod of Moses, had eaten up all other questions, and the old question of Re-former and Conservative is done away with. He had been called a party-man and he was one, hitherto he had done all in his power to oust the present Administration—(cries of question)—but now so little was he a party-man, as regards the old names—

Mr. FERRES would like to know if the ques-tion before the Convention was annexation?

Mr. McDONALD was astonished at the un-easiness gentlemen seemed to feel whenever the question of paramount importance was ap-proached. No one could accuse him of having any great respect for the members of the present Administration—especially not for Messrs Cam-eron and Hincks, yet if there was an election to-morrow, he would rather vote to keep those men in power for ever than he would vote for his own brother if he was an annexationist. (Great cheering.) Far from trying to oust the pre-sent Ministry. if he thought they were sincere in their attachment to British connexion, and he perceived by the *Montreal Gazette* that they were showing some signs of sincerity—(hear, hear)—if he thought they would be loyal—if they could only remain in place, he would go home, quit the League, and retire for ever from politi-cal life. The passion of his life was British con-nexion, and to build up this country so as to be *something* hereafter, and not to be merged in the States, and its inhabitants to be called "Ca-nucks" by the Yankees. He desired that we should remain attached to British connection till we can take care of ourselves, and become a people, a nation. (Cheers.) At the ratio in which our population is now increasing, we shall have 10,000,000 of people in half a century, and we shall then have attained the full stature of manhood, and be able to take our place among the nations of the earth. (Cheers.)

Mr. MURNEY said, that at the last meeting of the Convention, all that had been said to-day in favor of an elective Legislative Council was urged most strongly—the abuse of the prerogative of the Crown—the total prostration of the independence of the Upper House—the election by the people making it still more conservative than at present, all was urged in favor of the principle. On the other side it was argued, that, although for the present by the introduction of new members the body might have for a time thrown aside their independence—that as soon as they began to feel their position they would become the most conservative branch of the Legislature. He (Mr. Murney) was one of those who took that view, and that was the view of the majority of the Convention, and the proposal was negatived. He would ask what had occurred since that time to induce members to change their minds,—although he found that some who were then opposed to it, were now willing to make the change. He looked on it as done out of deference to those members of the Convention who were avowed annexationists. (Loud cries of hear, hear, and no, no.) He looked on it as an installment towards annexation. (Cheers, and no, no.) The next instalment would be to make the head of the Government elective, and the third instalment would be the total independence of the country, which would throw us into the vortex of annexation. (Cheers, and no, no.) At Kingston the proposal was rejected, and the Convention adopted three points for public discussion, viz., Protection to Native Industry, Retrenchment in the public Expenditure, and a Union of the Provinces. He asked, had these questions been agitated? Had the members of the Convention gone through their several counties to prepare the public mind? If not, why not agitate the country upon them, and await a general election? Not three months after the last Convention, annexation became the all-engrossing topic, and immediately following that change the Convention was called together. Were they called together for the purpose of again taking up the subject of this resolution? He thought not. It appeared to him that the express object of this meeting was to quiet and tranquilize the public mind, by adopting an immediate declaration against the views set forth in the Montreal manifesto, and yet they had been in session since Thursday, and had not had any resolution introduced touching on the subject. He should oppose both the original resolution and the amendment.

Mr. GEORGE DUGGAN would support the original resolution (loud cries of "hear, hear."). Instead of talking about their loyalty, and contradicting treasonable documents sent forth from the city of Montreal or elsewhere, he understood the business of the Convention was to consider the state of the country; and as they had already done so, and declared the country to be in such a state as it cannot continue in, their next duty was to propose to the people some means to redress that state of things. The men who composed the Convention needed to make no declaration of loyalty; they had given proofs of their loyalty far more expressive than any declaration could be. It would be mere child's play to tell the people of Canada we are loyal; our business is to point out the evils under which the country suffers, and suggest a remedy. He was in favour of the resolution, because it was only in unison with what the Convention had already declared. They had declared that they wanted larger powers of government, that our constitution is unsuited to us, and that we cannot go on under it in peace and prosperity. What particular dread could there be in the name of elective institutions? Why should they shrink from it? If they had confidence that there was sufficient intelligence and good sense in the people of the country to manage their own affairs, why should they send across the Atlantic to get the colonial secretary to determine who are the men with most experience and information to manage our business? (Cheers.) It was utterly inconsistent with all they had been saying and doing. They were asking from Great Britain enlarged powers; they should also seek to remove the Legislative Council, which has totally and entirely failed in the object contemplated by its creation. It was intended to be a conservative branch of the government, but what do we find it? We find it one of the worst species of democracy—a tool in the hands of the party who for the moment have obtained power in the province. It has assisted to pass laws which have thrown the whole province into disorder; and then we have been told by the representative of the Sovereign, as a reason for assenting to those laws, that they were passed by both branches of the legislature; and yet, when it was thought necessary to remove the seat of government to Toronto, because the head of the government had rendered himself so contemptible and obnoxious that he dared not be seen in the city of Montreal, the opinion of the Legislative Council was set aside, because they decided that the proposed step was improper and inexpedient, and no statesman-like reason had been adduced for it. Were he (Mr. D.) a member of the Legislative Council, he should feel himself a contemptible creature if his opinion was to be set aside and despised, whenever it suited the colonial secretary or the head of the government (hear, hear). The thing was a monstrous absurdity—the creation in this country of the very worst species of democracy. Compare that body with the House of Lords, indeed! Is the House of Lords made up by the political party in power for the time being? No; you have there hereditary legislators—sons, grandsons, great-grandsons, generation after generation, taking their seats there because their fathers held seats there—men of standing and property in the community. But that house cannot be crammed and its whole character altered at the mere whim of the ministry for the time being. Such a thing could not be done in England; it would create a revolution in the country if the ministry were to cram the upper house with their Sam Millses to carry rebel bills; the people of England would rise up in arms against it, and the noblemen who compose the house would raise their united voices also, and drive the ministers who attempted it from the councils of their sovereign. But here, the opinion of the Legislative Council is appealed from to that of the lower house, and the assent of the Assembly is a plea for any act, however absurd, injurious, contemptible and unjust (hear, hear). What was there to be frightened at in the term "elective"? What is it that will promote the peace and happiness of this country? Is it by taking the power of judging and considering their own business out of the hands of the people? They must not be guided by prejudice in this matter; they saw the country laid almost in ruins before them, and they had to devise some scheme to amend its position, and this was one of the remedies that suggested themselves. The men elected to the Legislative Council must have a high property qualification or a large stake in the country, and the electors also might be required to have a property qualification. He was not to be told that this was the same thing which created the rebellion which they rose to put down. We must progress step by step; we must seek what the people of the country require, be it elective institutions or anything else. (Hear, hear.) You must meet the wishes of the country, and the great way to stop the annexation movement is to give them full power of controuling their own affairs; the people of this country are not willing to give up the power of managing their own affairs into foreign hands or into the hands of those at a distance. He did not think it at all followed that because they had an elective Legislative Council based on a property qualification, that they must therefore have an elective Governor. But if the people of this colony would prefer an elective Governor, and think it would promote their happiness and prosperity, it would not be right for Great Britain to refuse it. Let it be pointed out to Great Britain that we are fit for the exercise of all the power we ask, it cannot be for her interest or her honor to withhold that power from us. (Cheers.) He would support the resolution, because he conceived it to be consistent with true Conservative principles of patriotism.

Mr. GLASSFORD opposed the amendment in a few words that were inaudible at the reporter's table.

Mr. VANKOUGHNET had not intended addressing the Convention on this subject, but as his name had been specially mentioned by Mr. Wilson, he felt it due to himself to explain the views he entertained. He did not think, that in considering the question of an elective Le-

gislative Council now, they were doing any thing inconsistent with what they did at Kingston, because, when the subject was broached at Kingston, it was before the Union of the Provinces had been discussed or agreed to. The question of an elective Legislative Council was brought forward with regard to the Province of Canada, and he (Mr. V.) opposed it on these two simple grounds—that as a resolution regarding a Union of the Provinces was to be brought forward, it would be useless to discuss the question of the constitution, or the construction of the Legislative Council of Canada; and he could not support the project of an elective Legislative Council for Canada, because no one was prepared to show how, Canada remaining as she is, you could constitute such an elective Legislative Council. The question came before them therefore in quite a different shape now from what it did at Kingston. Mr. Murney said, that he considered that those who would now support an elective Legislative Council, were doing so out of deference to the opinions of the annexationists. As far as he (Mr. Vankoughnet) was concerned, he had formed his opinions on this question, not with any reference to the opinions of any annexationist, or in consequence of any conference with Messrs. Wilson, Gamble, Gowan, or any one else; the views he would endeavour to enunciate were the result of reasoning in his own mind, not the result of arguments heard from any one, or from any desire in any way to yield: one iota to any one in favour of annexation, for with respect to that, he would state with Mr. MacDonald that if the only means of preventing annexation would be to make Mr. Baldwin Governor General of Canada for life, and sweep away every popular institution, he would vote to bring that about, —nor would he go for any measure of any description which he could be made to believe would lead to annexation, so much did he abhor the thought of tearing down Old England's flag and uprearing that of the United States. (Loud cheers.) He would now proceed to mention the reasons for which he was in favour of affirming the principle of an elective Legislative Council. He considered the present Legislative Council to be elective, and for this reason—He would ask the experience of any gentleman present whether or not the Crown of England could, under the system of responsible government conceded to these colonies, or would dare to take upon itself the responsibility of appointing to the Legislative Council any member whose appointment had not the sanction of the Provincial ministry in power? The Imperial Government might refuse to appoint a man whom the Provincial Government might recommend, but it would never assume to itself the responsibility of appointing to the Legislative Council, any individual whom the Provincial Government might not approve of. It must therefore be admitted as a truism that the local ministry of the day appoint the Legislative Council, and that the Sovereign simply confirms their nomination. Gentlemen might say, that they merely nominate, not elect them, but it was a mere quibble about words, because the thing means the same: If they nominate and the Sovereign confirms the nomination, then they elect them. The ministry then, for their own selfish objects, and not the party for the time being in the majority, have been in the habit of electing the Legislative Council; and he was of opinion that, under a confederated union of the British North American Provinces, we could procure an elective Legislative Council of a better description than what the ministry have hitherto been in the habit of sending to Parliament. Before going further, he would allude to the construction of the British House of Lords; in that respect we have no transcript of the British constitution here, and it was because he felt this, that he felt there was no weight in the argument that they were defiling the British constitution in adopting a measure at variance with its character. The present mode of appointing the Legislative Council is not in accordance with the constitution of the House of Lords. There the appointment is not merely an appointment made by the party in power, or by the Crown, but there is a class which enjoys the hereditary honour of sitting in that House—a class with which the Crown cannot interfere—a class which becomes, from the fact of being hereditary, totally irrespective of the Crown—which stands between the Crown and the people; and although the Crown exercises the privilege of appointing members to the House of Lords, would any one tell him that the Crown of England could ever think of appointing two hundred Lords to that House for the purpose of swamping the hereditary influence of those who have been there before? (Loud cries of hear, hear) But we have no hereditary honors or descent in Canada—all our members of the Legislative Council go there as the nominees of a party, and they are sent there by the Crown for the purpose of advancing certain political views, just as the Crown have given Lord Elgin a peerage because they wanted some one to match Lord Stanley as a speaker, and Lord Elgin is an orator; that, he was told, was the purpose for which Lord Elgin had been made a Peer, and for a similar reason parties in power here will send Legislative Councillors to Parliament. He was aware that these Councillors would in time forget the purposes for which they were sent there, and become more independent than those who sent them there intended, but for some time after they went there they would act as mere party men. Now, he (Mr. Vankoughnet) was in favour of an elective Legislative Council if there was a confederated union of the Provinces, but under no other circumstances; all he intended to confirm by voting for the resolution was, that if there was a union of the British North American Provinces a way might be devised by which the Legislative Council should be elected; if it should be found that such a union was not feasible, he did not conceive that he should be committed to the principle of an elective Legislative Council for Canada—he was only affirming that under a confederated union of the Provinces, a mode might be devised of obtaining an elective Legislative Council better than the present mode of obtaining it, which he considered to be defective. The resolution only admits that there may be circumstances in which an elective Legislative Council may be obtained. The mode in which it was to be elected would be matter for discussion hereafter. Mr. Wilson and one party might be in favour of electing them by the people, he and another party by the local Parliaments, and if they could not come into one another's views an elective Legislative Council would become impossible. But now supposing there was a confederated union of the British North American Provinces, supposing that each Province has its local Parliament, and that there is a general Legislature for the Confederation exercising certain powers over the whole; it was to that Legislature that he would send the elective Councillors, and he would send them in this way: he would allow the local Parliaments to elect the Councillors—(Hear, hear)—and when he was told that he was infringing on the British Constitution and introducing a system entirely different from the present one, he would answer no, because bearing in mind that the party in power for the time sends the Legislative Councillors to Parliament, and admitting that all the local Parliaments might, by a majority, entertain precisely the same opinions as the Ministry holding the reins of confederated power—admitting that, he would ask the Convention, he would ask any man of calm dispassionate sense, whether he would rather that the Councillors should come from the local Parliaments, even supposing these local Parliaments to entertain precisely the same opinions with the Ministry holding the confederated power, than simply from the Ministry themselves? Whether he does not think that the body of the party which gives the Ministry its position is much more likely to be honest than the Ministry themselves? Because, although the ministry and party may hold sentiments in unison, the ministry will have selfish objects in view which their party have not—objects of place and power—and will sometimes deceive their party by getting them to support measures in Parliament, the effect of which that party may not see, though the ministry may have a covert object in getting it passed. He did not think the party could be *less* honest than the ministry, and there was a great chance of their being *more* honest. Then again, supposing there was a confederated union, and that we had the same Parliament in Canada as we have now, and that Messrs Sam Mills and Sam Crane were members of the Canadian Parliament, did they believe that when the Parliament was called upon to send members to the Legislative Council of the Confederated Union, that they would select Mr. Sam Mills or Mr. Sam Crane, or men of that stamp and calibre in every respect, to remain there for double the time perhaps that the Assembly would continue to exist? No, they would have some respect for their own character, and would not, like the ministry, be actuated by a desire to send men to the Legislative Council to carry out certain views and measures. He was opposed to electing the Legislative Council directly from the people, and he opposed Mr. Wilson's resolution at Kingston on the ground, that he did not see how it could be done, but if there was a Confederated Union of the Provinces they could be nominated by the local Legislatures, and you could not, by that means, get worse members than the ministry would give you, indeed there would be more chance from the differences of opinion that would exist in the local Parliaments, of collecting a body of independent men in the Confederated Legislative Council. Mr. McDonald said that it would interfere with the principles of responsible government. He (Mr. V.) thought that he had shown that under the principles of responsible government, the ministry of the day must elect the Legislative Council. If it be necessary that under responsible government the Legislative Council must always agree with the popular branch of the Legislature, what was the use of having it at all? The object, as they all agreed, was to have a check; but how could it be a check, if it was necessary that there should be such men always appointed as should agree with the Legislative Assembly? He could not see the force of the argument, that they were interfering with the principles of the British constitution, because he denied that we have a transcript of the British constitution, as we have no hereditary peerage. But he would admit the force of the argument—and that was what actuated him in this Convention—that there was a terrible danger in laying a rash hand on the ark of our constitution. No one felt the grave responsibility more than he did; he would exercise the utmost caution; he would do nothing rashly in a question of such vital importance, affecting the character of our institutions; and although he was in favour of an elective Legislative Council when a confederated union of the provinces should give us the material, yet he must confess that he would rather, until that union had been formed, and until he saw upon what principles it was formed, postpone the question of an elective Legislative Council. But when he was told that delay was impossible, and that he must make up his mind one way or the other, he was not afraid or ashamed, after due consideration, to declare his opinions and take action on them (cheers).

Mr. HATT was willing to admit that the grossest means had been used in packing the Legislative Council, but he could not consent, nor did he think the majority of the Convention would consent to change entirely the nature of that body. He believed the great majority of the Convention desired to remain under monarchical institutions; well, if they desired to do that, and to alter the constitution so as to admit of their living under that Government, they must ask themselves the question—if the remedy proposed to-day was consistent with that Go-

vernment? He held not; he held that if they admitted that it was necessary to make the Legislative Council elective, they would do it because the power of the Crown had been abused in the packing of that body. If they did this, they could not stop there. (Hear, hear.) If they had not confidence in the Crown to appoint Legislative Councillors, they had not confidence in the Crown to appoint the Governor, or the Judges. (Loud cries of hear, hear.) They would have to make all their officers elective. (Hear.) Now he would ask the Convention if they were prepared to do that, or if it was compatible with the institutions under which they were living, that they should have the elective principle. (Cheers.) He was surprised to see men who had been long in the province—men like Mr. Gowan, rise in the Convention, and advocate the very measures which MacKenzie and Papineau advocated. If Messrs. Papineau and MacKenzie had succeeded in getting an elective Legislative Council, we should have had the principles of the 92 Resolutions fully carried out. Why did the Rebellion take place? Was it not because Mackenzie applied to the Colonial office, so much denounced, amongst other things for this very measure of an elective Legislative Council, and would not be listened to? And now they are following in his very steps! (Loud cries of hear, hear.) Every step he took made him more and more opposed to the elective principle. It had been instanced by Mr. Gowan that the Wardens of the different Districts, elected by the people, were Conservatives. It might be so, but he (Mr. Hatt) would be sorry to see the Legislative Council of this Province altogether Conservative; he would like to see that body composed of honest and consistent men, and men who had a stake in the country, be they Reformers or Conservatives; there were men whom he would like to see in that Council, who had been consistent Reformers all their lives, but who had an opinion of their own, and a stake in the country, and would legislate not for party purposes, but for what they conceived to be for the best interests of the country. The Wardens of the Districts had been referred to, but with one or two exceptions, he did not think they were the kind of men he would like to see in the Legislative Council; they have neither the position in the country, nor the property qualification necessary. It was for these reasons that he was opposed to the elective principle, and he implored the Convention to pause before making a declaration in favour of a measure which he sincerely believed to be incompatible with monarchical institutions. (Hear, hear, and no, no.) The reason this elective Legislative Council now asked for, was because they were for the moment out of power. (No, no.) He was convinced it was the case, and yet if they went to the country on the measures which have been adopted by the party in power, which have done so much to ruin the Constitution of the country, he felt satisfied the country would not approve of these measures. He would rather appeal to the country on the measures which had been determined on by the Convention, than attempt to alter the Constitution; for once begin and there was no telling where they might stop. (Cheers.)

Mr. D'ARCY BOULTON said, that although they had received a little light upon some points, the subject was still surrounded with darkness When he spoke of the light they had received he alluded to the explanation given by Mr. Vankoughnet, of the extent to which the resolution was intended to go. He (Mr. B.) had no idea till he heard that, of the view taken by the gentleman who moved the resolution. Mr. Vankoughnet's speech had much strengthened his opposition to the measure, because he had told them there were many views that might be taken of the matter, and that if he was not certain that the view he takes would be acted on he would oppose it. Now he (Mr. B.) thought that they ought not to interfere with the principles of the Constitution, unless they were perfectly sure of the course they were adopting. The intention of the mover of the resolution appeared to him to be that the Council shall be elected by the people.

Mr. WILSON rose to explain that, if Mr. Boulton had been present at the time he opened the discussion, he would have learned that he did not propose that the Council should be elected by the people, he had suggested that it should be elected by the different Municipalities, or Corporations.

Mr. AIKMAN, who had seconded Mr. Dixon's amendment as originally submitted, here intimated that he had not seconded the amendment now before them.

Mr. BOULTON said, that if it was merely intended to establish a Council out of the various Legislative Assemblies of the united provinces he would cheerfully accede to it, but he did not see anything on the face of the resolution that would give the people of the country to understand that that was the object contemplated by the Convention.

The Chairman here intimated that as Mr. Dixon's amendment had not found a seconder, it must drop, whereupon

Mr. MURNEY moved the following amendment seconded by CAPT. YOUNG, of Hillier:—

That it is inexpedient for this Convention to recommend to the people of Canada any change in the present constitution of this Colony. That in addition to its former address, a further declaration be made public of its disapproval of the Montreal Manifesto in favour of annexation of this Province to the United States, and of its determination to agitate those questions already before the public, which in the opinion of this Convention, will ameliorate our condition without endangering the connection with the Mother Country.

He would remark that, he had heard nothing yet to convince him that any change in the constitution was needed, and he was certain that even although members were sent into the Council for party purposes, they would in a short time feel their own dignity, and their entire independence of the Crown. He was opposed to any change in our present constitution, he thought it would work well; and he thought they should be satisfied in endeavouring to obtain the things

which they had declared in their declaration to be necessary in order to promote the prosperity of the country.

Mr. BOULTON, then continued his remarks. They had been told by the mover of the resolution that it was intended only to comprehend a Council elected by the various constituent bodies of those states composing the federation of the British Provinces. Well, if that were embodied in the resolution, and if it went forth to the people of the country, that it was a very moderate extension of the elective principle that they desired, he should be satisfied; he thought that would be an admirable mode of obtaining a Legislative Council for the confederation of the Provinces, but that was not conveyed in the resolution; the resolution would lead to the belief that the Convention wished to extend the franchise to the people, and the same would be gathered by the arguments made use of by the supporters of the resolution? Had not Mr. Gowan told the Convention that those of the old British Colonies that enjoyed the elective principle most fully, were the most continuing in their attachment to the British Crown, and that for that reason he wished to liberalize our institutions, and give the people themselves the power of forming the Legislative Council—did that accord with the explanation now given by the mover of the resolution? He was satisfied that if they attempted to make any innovation on the Constitution of the country, which the majority of the people revere, they would only get themselves into disgrace, and injure their influence among the people of the country, when they left the Convention to go amongst them. In his district the people were opposed to the elective principle, and he believed that the people of the Province generally would regard the proposed change as impolitic and uncalled for. He denied altogether that our position at the present time was at all analagous to that of the old American colonies at the time they revolted; there never was a country on the face of the globe where the majority of the people had more freedom under the Constitution than the people living in British North America at this moment; the British Government is not imposing on us laws contrary to our feelings and interests. The only thing they had to complain of was that they were in a minority. (No, no, no.) He repeated that they were in a minority in the country at the present moment. [Loud cries of no, no.] As the Conservative body, they were in a minority. [No, no, and a voice, "we are not Conservatives."] They were supposed to represent the Conservatives of the country, and the Conservatives were certainly in a minority. [Loud cries of no, no.] He did not mean to be understood that they were there for the purpose of fostering the Conservative party, he repudiated the idea, but as Conservatives they had left their respective constituencies, and they were supposed to carry out the feelings of the Conservatives of the country, and be conservators of the Constitution under which they lived. [Hear, hear.] He believed there was not a single Reformer in the Convention. It would be impolitic to adopt this resolution, unless they wished the country to understand what Mr. Duggan maintained the resolution intended, that they were liberalizing the Constitution, and extending the franchise they at present enjoy. When they called upon the people at the hustings to make the Ministry responsible for their misdeeds, let them not put it in their power to say, you have been tinkering the Constitution of the country, and making changes which the country never contemplated. Some gentlemen said they wished to make the Constitution more democratic, but would they increase the power of the people by carrying out this resolution in the way contemplated by Mr. Vankoughnet? No, it would be only giving them the same power to carry on the government, only in a different way. He concluded by urging the Convention not to take up the subject of the elective principle at all on the present occasion, as by so doing they would be endangering the influence they already possessed with the country, and by passing this resolution, only holding out hopes to the people which they never intended should be realized.

Mr. McKechnie rose for the purpose of supporting the original resolution, (Cheers,) and in so doing, he thought that they were proceeding upon constitutional principles; they were advocating that which they had the power to advocate within the bounds of the constitution, —it was on that principle that he supported the original resolution, (Cheers.) He was one of those who believed that the British Constitution, as we have it now, and as it has existed in all times, was one of the most wonderful constitutions for adapting itself to all circumstances and to all states. He firmly believed that it had this power of adaptation.— He did not consider that constitution as we have it here, to be time-honoured; he did not consider that we need be so awfully alarmed at laying our hands on what was called "the ark of our constitution. (Loud cries of "Hear, hear.") Our constitution, as he understood it, was the Union Act. (Hear, hear.) Was there anything time-honoured about that? (Cheers) Was there anything dreadful in laying our hands on an act passed only the other day? (Hear, hear.) He advocated the original resolution upon the ground that he believed it was perfectly competent to this body, and he believed they were sent there for that purpose. to take into consideration the evils under which we are now suffering, and that this resolution was a remedy, which he felt convinced would alleviate many of those evils. (Cheers.) He would cite authorities for the statement he had made, that the elective democratic principle was one perfectly within the bounds of the British Constitution. It was one which had been granted by Charles II., a monarch infinitely more absolute in his authority than our Queen is to-day. He held in his hand the charter granted by him, giving a constitution to the State of Connecticut. It commences this way—"With regard to the powers of the Government, it conferred on the colonists un-

qualified power to govern themselves; they were allowed to elect all their own officers, (Cheers,) to enact their own laws, to administer justice without appeal to England; to inflict punishment and to confer pardon, and in a word, to exercise every power deliberative and active. (Loud cheers.)—The King, far from reserving a negative on the acts of the colony, did not even require that laws should be transmitted for his inspection; and no provision was made for the interference of the English Government in any event whatever. (Cheers.) From the first, the minds of the yeomanry were kept active by the exercise of the elective franchise, and except under James 11. there was no such thing in the land as an officer appointed by the English King." (Loud cheers.)

A Delegate.—What is your authority?

Mr. McKechnie.—The authority was an unimpeachable one, Bancroft's History of the United States. (Ironical cheers and laughter.) Gentlemen would understand that what he had read from, was a distinct and succinct account of the charter granted to the Colony, and he need only mention the name of Mr. Bancroft, a man eminent in literature, and lately United States ambassador in England. (Hear, hear.) He had quoted the charter for the purpose of showing that the elective principle had been granted before to British Colonies, which he considered it essential to do for the sake of those who think we are to act on British practice. Having established that fact, the next question was how far this elective system is adapted to the state of society in which we live. (Hear, hear.) He conceived that they had never heard of a more purely democratic community than our own. He did not know that there was any part of the world in which there was more equality as to the position in life and circumstances of our existence than in this Colony. He contended that the tendencies of this community are as democratic as they can be. Lord Durham and every other statesman had stated that it was so. Lord Durham in his report as much as states that it is impossible for this community to be other than a democracy. These two points being established, that they were advocating nothing but what they were entitled to do, without interfering with the honoured institutions of their forefathers, and that this is a purely democratic community, then comes the question how far the present state of the Province requires a change to an elective form of Government. The impure state of the Legislative Council, and the influences exercised on it so as to make it merely a repetition of the Legislative Assembly, had been distinctly acknowledged by almost every gentleman who had spoken, he need not; therefore, take up the time of the Convention in again going over that ground. He should, therefore, take it for granted that the state of the Legislative Council is at present evil, and is one that requires a change, and although they might be obnoxious to the objection that they were an association of tinkers, ready to tinker the constitution, yet they could not get over the fact that here was an evil which they were required to cure. He would be happy if he could say that there was no evil, and that no change was required, but was it not apparent to all, that a change was demanded. (Hear, hear.) Then comes the question, what change shall be made? The learned gentlemen who last spoke, cast a slur on the advocates of this resolution, by saying it was a tinkering resolution. There was no disposition to tinker at the Constitution, they were only advocating a principle which they conceived to be perfectly within the bounds of that constitution, on the sacred ark' of which he (Mr. Boulton) had asserted they were about to lay their hands. The only change he believed to be possible, was to have the Legislative Council elective. (Hear, hear.) He (Mr. McKechnie) did not entirely agree with the resolution. He would go further than the resolution. He did not wish to lead the Convention on further than they were aware of; he was there to advocate a constitution similar to that granted to Connecticut—an entirely Democratic constitution. (Loud and continued cheering in the house and gallery.) He was for introducing the elective principle into the upper house; the details of the change would have to be settled by a higher power. Having thus endeavoured to point out the necessity for the change now recommended, he next came to the point, that he believed it was one of those changes which were about to perpetuate the connection of this country with Great Britain for time immemorial, (cheers) He was convinced that if this change were not made, demagogues would always be pointing out the inferiority of our position to that of the neighbouring republic, (cheers) From what he knew of the feelings and aspirations of the people of this country, he was convinced that unless they were given such power, within the bounds of the Constitution, as would enable them to feel that they have nothing to desire, you would always leave open some loop-hole for demagogues to go upon, (hear, hear.) He should conclude by simply stating that he conceived the change they were seeking was a perfectly constitutional change—a change, which as British freemen, with the evidence before them, they had a right to ask, because they had a precedent for it. He supported it because he considered it a change best adapted to our present state of society, and that if it was brought before the people it would turn their minds from the contemplation of other and more dreadful ills to which demagogues had directed them, and which, if not checked, would ultimately drive us into independence, or into the arms of the republic which is delicately and coyly waiting for us on the other side, (cheers and laughter.) Firmly convinced that unless the elective principle was adopted in the government of the country, we should be a lost Colony to Great Britain, he should vote for it. Mr. McKechnie resumed his seat amidst loud cheering.

Mr. A. J. McDonell supported the amendment, because if the elective system was once adopted we must carry it through all parts of our constitution, and its adoption would lead us into the road to Republicanism. On this ground he opposed it. If they once began to tinker with the constitution, they might depend upon it the people of the country would think that republicanism was their aim. He was opposed to any alteration in the constitution, and he thought they could secure the independence of the Legislative Council without making it subservient either to the people or to the Ministry. He thought it would be more consistent with the wishes of their constituents if, instead of pursuing Mr. Wilson's course, they were to seek to limit the number of members who compose the Legislative Council. (Hear hear.) He thought, moreover, that the indignation which the recent packing of that body had created throughout the country, would render any future Ministry, whether Reformers or Conservatives, cautious how they meddle with the constitution. There never was a grosser outrage inflicted on any people than the suppression of the independence of the upper house, but he was of opinion that the evil had worked its own cure; it had made the people reflect and cry out for a change, not by doing away with the Legislative Council altogether, but by placing some check on the undue influence which the Crown exercises over it. The Constitutions conferred on Rhode Island and Connecticut had been instanced by Mr. Gowan and others as an argument in favour of the course they were seeking to adopt, but in his (Mr. McD.'s) opinion they afforded no argument. Rhode Island and Connecticut were in a very different position than we are; they were merely proprietary establishments, they had no general bearing on the British empire, no influence on the position of the British empire. At the time Great Britain granted those constitutions to Rhode Island and Connecticut, it was a matter of little importance whether they enjoyed the fullest liberty of electing their Governor and Council or not, because the Governor and Council of Rhode Island did not act so much on the British empire as the Mayor and Corporation of the city of Toronto, but the Governor and Legislative Council of British America have some bearing on the empire. We have become too important for Great Britain to give us up because they have no pecuniary interest in retaining us. Great Britain retains these Colonies not for any commercial or political advantage she derives from us, but in order to maintain her scale in the rank of nations; England will never give up these Colonies as long as she wishes to remain a first rate power. If they adopted the scheme of an elective Legislative Council, they must go on to elect their own Governor, and then he would ask what would be the connection between Great Britain and Canada? England must have the power of appointing a Governor over this Colony, if it was only to keep up the semblance of power. (Cheers and counter cheers.) The Colonists must feel that there is some connecting link between them and England; it must not be a mere idea.

Mr. Gowan.—Who appoints the Governor General of India? (Loud cries of Hear, hear.)

Mr. McDonell thought that was a very different thing, but he maintained that we must have some agent here from Great Britain, holding some power to enable us to feel that we are still connected with Great Britain. [Ironical Cheers.] He considered that if they agreed to Mr. Wilson's motion, they must go further, and deprive Great Britain of every semblance of power, and on that ground he called upon all who were desirous of maintaining the connection to aid him in opposing it. Let them not "at one fell swoop" go in for this change, for which the people of the country are not prepared. He for one was not prepared for it; nor had he heard any arguments adduced to convince either him or the people of the country that the great change was desirable. He had heard in this Convention sneering allusions to Canadian loyalty, but he maintained that though the sentiment of loyalty might have been dimmed and nearly destroyed by the payment of rebels and the state to which the country was reduced, yet it was not extinct; we must still feel that we are connected with the greatest empire in the world, and have had some hand in civilizing the nations, and spreading abroad the light and truth of the gospel. [Cheers.] A change in our institutions once allowed, would lead to endless conflicts; he believed that the passing of this resolution would lead to an elective Governor, then to Independence, and from Independence to Annexation. [Cheers.] Let them limit the number of the Legislative Council to half that of the Assembly and appoint them for life, and they would by that means obtain an independent body. One argument urged by Mr. Vankoughnet was, that the Crown would never interfere with the Colonial ministers in the appointment of Legislative Councillors. He would remind the Convention that the Crown did interfere in one instance, and in one that did great credit, and showed how much better able the Crown was to appoint members than the Provincial Ministry. It was the Crown that appointed the Hon. William Henry Draper to the Upper House, as a reward for his distinguished talents, and that too after the House of Assembly had declared that the Hon. Robt. Baldwin should be Attorney General [Hear hear.] If they had a few more such members as that, the Legislative Council would be a very different body from what it is at present. [Cries of hear, hear and question.]

Mr. Mack then rose and said, that as usual in the meetings of the League, a great deal had been said upon every motion that had come before them, that appeared to be very extraneous to the question, and although he would not take upon himself to say this, for the purpose of throwing a censure on the method in which the business was carried on, he made the remark for the purpose of protesting against many remarks, made against those who sup-

ported the side he took—in favour of the original motion. (Cheers.) It had been said a dozen times, that whatever was done in this matter, was done by those who were in favour of Annexation themselves, or who wished to conciliate the annexationists. (Hear, hear.) He protested against such a construction being put on the conduct of those, who wished to carry out the measures of amelioration, which he conceived are involved in Mr. Wilson's resolutions. It had been asked by one gentleman, why was the Convention brought together here? He [Mr. Mack] was surprised at that question, because he thought that if they looked back on the circumstances that brought them together some three months ago, the reason must be apparent. It was then known and felt that there was a great degree of dissatisfaction with the conduct of the Imperial Government towards the Colony. It arose because they found that this constitution of which they had heard so much to-day, had been trampled upon; because they thought that the interference in certain circumstances by the Imperial Government, had produced results of the most disastrous kind; but it remained for them to see during the last few weeks, the Montreal manifesto make its appearance, when they saw annexation take its start from a much different and much less noble cause; and he who asserted that the principle and the desire for annexation to the United States, was not gaining ground, was either wilfully blind in his prejudices, or could know nothing whatever of the state of this country. [Loud cheers] It was as a loyal and honest subject that he would support all the resolutions brought forward by Mr. Wilson, because he honestly and verily believed that, by affirming such resolutions, England could conserve our loyalty consistently with our liberties; [loud cheers] he hoped he should not be falling into the same mistake of travelling from the record, if he compared the annexation movement as it existed when they met at Kingston with the annexation movement as it exists now. The first arose from what were conceived to be serious grievances; the present is a desire for annexation, that arises from £ s d. There was nothing that had ever pointed, with a more prophetic finger, to the downfall of a nation, than when men measure their loyalty by their pockets. [Cheers.]— Rome and Greece both fell, when loyalty to their country and true patriotism became matters of mere £ s d. The argument for annexation in the Montreal manifesto, was nothing more than that by being united to those States, we shall find our property increased in value, our laws improved, French influence destroyed, (which is the only reason sometimes given in the Lower Province,) it was nothing but profit. When Esau sold his birth-right he had his mess of pottage offered him, but the Montreal manifesto only held out promises, which may never be fulfilled. He would ask if our neighbours are not trading with our produce? Are our cities not increasing from year to year? has Montreal not increased during the last ten years more in proportion than any city in the United States? not in laths and plaster, and green paint, but in solid stone, which will look like everything else British, when the clapboards of America have been swept to more convenient places. (Laughter.) Was he, holding sentiments like these, likely to do anything that would lead to annexation? He protested to his GOD that he wanted some better reason for forgetting his allegiance, than this mess, which was only promised. He did not envy the hearts, although he might respect the judgment, of the men who could offer for this promised mess, to sell their fellow citizens to these dealers in black blood. (Loud cheers.) But, feeling that this annexation movement was gaining ground, feeling the ground of his allegiance shaken under his feet by these annexationists, it was to save the flag of Old England that he would ask her to make him freer and he would be loyal still. (Cheers.) They had declared yesterday against Downing street interference, they had affirmed that principle, and how could they refuse to follow it out—they would be straining at the gnat while they swallowed the camel. Such interference, and such continued interference in our affairs, as we have lately seen, was not to be endured; it was injurious to us as freemen, it was injurious to us as British subjects, and, if persisted in, would throw us into the arms of the United States (Loud cheers.) He supported the resolution because he believed that, by England granting us the remedial measures it seeks, these colonies may continue British long after our heads are laid in the soil (Cheers.) It was in vain that his eloquent and learned friend, Mr. Vankoughnet, had said you must be cautious, and let no impious hand touch the ark of our constitution. That ark of the constitution had been rudely shaken, and it was because recent events had shewn that we have no British constitution here, that he would like to see measures of this kind brought forward, that we might have a form of constitution that would enable us to continue British. Who should tell him that we have the British Constitution in Canada?—who shou'd tell him that we have the system of checks which that constitution provides. What is the Governor General?—a receptacle of £7,500 a year and a dancer of Scotch reels! (Tremendous cheers and laughter.) What is the upper house? When he was young his friends used to teach him to believe, according to the doctrines of his church, that it was not the four walls of the building, but the people in it, that formed the church; but that doctrine is contradicted now, men seem to think that the Legislative Council is the four walls of a building in which men do the will of Baldwin and Lafontaine. (Cheers) There is no check in our present system, and he thought they would take the wisest, most effectual, and most British course, by making the upper house elective; and when the proper time came he should be prepared to vote for

making the Governor elective also. (Cheers.) He could not agree with those gentlemen who said that our constitution requires no change. We have no constitution; our task is now to make it. Neither could he agree with those who thought the course, they were proposing likely to lead to independence or annexation. He was not one of those who would vote for Baldwin himself as Governor, rather than see the British flag torn down. (Hear, hear.)—There was nothing of the spaniel in his composition. (Cheers.) He could not be licked into loyalty—he must have his full rights and liberties if he was to remain a British subject. The British constitution still exists, because it has been changing from time to time, and not because its time-honored institutions have been unchangeable, like the laws of the Medes and Persians, but because it has changed from day to day to suit itself to the altered times; it is not time honoured and revered, but presently honoured and revered. He [Mr. Mack] neither loved the Government of the past, nor should he love the Government of the future, but he would wish to love the Government under which he lived, because it was suited to the times. The system under which we live is not suited for freemen to live under, but he contended that these resolutions offer to England the means of securing what she has not got—our love, and they offer her more, they offer her the means of securing the love of freemen. [Loud cheers.]

Mr. HAMILTON thought the resolution consistent with the one adopted on Saturday. The resolution before the Convention had been supported and opposed on various grounds; one gentleman opposed it because it was inconsistent with Responsible Government, because it would at once bring into collision the elective Legislative Council and the Administration appointed by the Lower House. There would be a manifest inconsistency if it was to be adapted to the Government of the present province of Canada, but it should be borne in mind that the principle was to be adapted to a newly constituted geographical country, and that an entirely new constitution was to be framed for a new country.— He did not therefore think that the argument advanced on that subject should weigh against the resolution. He did not advocate this elective principle for the purpose of turning any Ministry out of power, but because he saw in it a principle consistent with reason, common sense, freedom, and the free exercise of the judgment of a free people, who know or ought to know, what is best for their political, commercial, and social interests, [Cheers.] It was because he worshipped that principle in every shape and form, that he should vote for the resolution. If a new constitution is to be established here, he would like to see it formed and based upon such principles as would command the respect, the love, and admiration of every man, whose judgment must be worth having; a government to be really firm and established, must have its hold in the hearts and affections of a loyal and contented people. They were asked, whither are you travelling on this downward path of destruction ? are you prepared to admit this demon of the elective principle into the constitution, to destroy you ? He would point the gentlemen who were so frightened at this creature of their imagination, this terrible vampire, that was to eat out all that is great and glorious in the constitution, to the constitution of the District Councils. When these Councils were first established it was proclaimed from one end of the province to the other, that the principle was a wild Democratic one, and one that would never answer. For the first few years in the Niagara District, politics were allowed to interfere, and men were sent to the Council for their political opinions alone, and collisions took place, but now all has come right, and the people are contented with having the management of their own affairs. At first the system was adopted of the Council nominating three men for the office of Clerk, and laying the names before the Government, but on one occasion the Government conferred the appointment on the man who had the smallest number of votes. The Council had no right to complain, as it was within the Prerogative of the Crown, but they repealed the by-law providing for the salary of the Clerk, and the effect was, that the very next Session of Parliament. the law was altered, so as to allow the Council to elect their own Clerk, and since that, there has been no dispute. The same might be said of the appointment of the Wardens and District Treasurers, and it was a proof of the ability of the people to elect their own officers, that the Councils had elected nearly the same men as Treasurers, as the Government appointed The elective principle had answered so well in Municipal affairs, that he thought it ought to be introduced into other branches of the Government, and he believed that if that was done, it would purify the Government of the country, and restore the people of this Province to the high position of integrity they ought to occupy. He was convinced that if the elective principle was more extensively and largely admitted into all our offices in the country, we should be better and more honestly served, and the demagogues through whom a corrupt administration can at any time rule, would be swept from the face of the country, and we would thus be freed from the vampires who are sapping the very life-blood of the Province. (Cheers.) It was because he knew and felt all this, that he was in favour of the elective principle, and not from any party motives; he repudiated such motives. There was no doubt that the passage of the Rebellion Losses Bill called the Convention into existence politically, but the commercial and agricultural depression had had some hand in calling them together. He did not believe that the people of Canada were panting and thirsting for this elective principle, but he believed they were panting for some form of Government in which they could have confidence, and he believed that a constitution like that proposed, having its foundation in the good sense and

integrity of the people, would secure its confidence. He had heard it contended by some that, because the prerogative of the Crown had been prostituted for the lowest of purposes, on some recent occasion, they should therefore do away with the Legislative Council altogether ; but that seemed to him like merging the larceny in the murder they would commit in the destruction of the body, and he did not believe in such a doctrine as that ; it was not the true principle on which they should go ; he had great pleasure in supporting the elective principle, because he believed it to be founded on reason and common sense, and that the people would never be satisfied without having a just and due proportion in the constitution for the Government of the country. [Cheers].

Mr D. B. READ briefly opposed both the motion and the amendment, amidst loud cries of question.

Mr. GAMBLE had listened with great attention to the debate, and he hoped he had made something by it, but he had also listened to a great deal that might have been left unsaid. He really did not think the gentleman who drew up the amendment could have known what he was writing, for here they had been complaining of all kinds of evils, and yet the amendment declared that it was inexpedient for the Convention to recommend any change in the Constitution. Now he would like to know if the Convention was prepared to adopt anything of that kind ? he for one was not. He was in favour of elective institutions, because he felt satisfied that they were the only means of retaining this colony as a dependency of the British Crown ; he was satisfied that nothing short of that would accomplish the end they had in view. He had heard gentlemen talk of their loyalty and allegiance and all that sort of thing, why of all the cant ever canted in this canting country, the cant of hypocrisy was the worst. [Loud and prolonged cheering] Talk about allegiance indeed ! He would yield to no man in allegiance, but gentlemen seemed to forget that allegiance has its rights, and that if fealty was required from the subject to the Sovereign, there are rights that ought to be yielded in return—to foster, uphold, and protect us. He was second to no man on the floor for that chivalrous feeling of loyalty that formerly possessed his breast, but, as Mr. Mack had observed, he was not like the spaniel, to endure kicks and buffeting, he felt that his loyalty was going—going—because his liberties had been invaded in a most atrocious manner. (Cheers.) Like Bob Acres' courage, it was oozing out—oozing out (Cheers and laughter). He was satisfied that, to retain this country a colony of Great Britain, a prosperous, free and happy people, the best course was, to adopt elective institutions, not only as proposed in the resolution before the Convention, that the Legislative Council should be elective, but that the election should emanate from the people, and that the Councils in the different Provinces themselves should be elective. They would thus be laying the foundation of good government; but he would not stop there, he would make the head of the government also elective. (Great cheering.) He would appeal to reason and common sense, and ask the gentlemen opposite to reflect on what had been the cause of the troubles and differences in this country Had they not arisen from the appointment of these two branches of the Legislature by the Crown of England. Mr. Read proposed as a remedy, that the number of Councillors should be limited, and said that would be sufficient; but what had been the cause of complaint year after year in this country? The Assemblies, both in Upper and Lower Canada, complained that the Legislative Councils were obstructives—that they could not get their measures through the Councils, which were necessary for the good of the country. Did they wish to perpetuate a system like that? He (Mr. Gamble) was as much an admirer as any man could be, of the British constitution; he believed it was one that adapts itself to the circumstances of the people, in an extraordinary manner, but he was satisfied that, in this country, the materials do not exist to form a transcript of the British constitution (Loud cries of hear, hear.) Look at the British House of Lords, composed of the most wealthy, the best educated, and the most intelligent people in the land—as fine a race of people as ever existed on the face of the earth; wealth, intelligence and education, have their influence, and that influence attaches itself to the body, but where are the materials in Canada from which to constitute a Council, to exercise the influence on the people, generally, that the House of Lords does in England?—[Hear, hear.] Well, if we have not the material, we must take the next best course we can pursue—one that has already proved successful. He would appeal to the state of the Municipal Councils from one end of the Province to the other, and ask, if the elective principle had not proved eminently successful there? (loud cries of hear, hear,) and if the elective system had answered so well in this instance, why not go a step further, and carry it into higher matters; he advocated this measure, because he was satisfied it was the only remedy that would save us from Annexation, and that, he wished to avoid. He believed that the scheme laid down by the Convention—the union of the Provinces, would place the country in a better position than it could possibly occupy under Annexation.—[Hear, hear.] If gentlemen desired that this country should be retained to the Crown of Great Britain, that we should have the old flag waving over us, it was not to be done by shifts and expedients. They must apply a remedy commensurate to the disease; the disease was acute, and before the Convention met again, Annexation would in all probability have made such large strides, that they would not be able to resist its progress. He advocated these measures, because he was convinced they would be most conducive to the welfare and prosperity of the country; but he advocated them also on another ground, namely: that they could not have any other institutions. [Hear, hear.] He would ask any gentleman present, what form of Government he thought would prevail in this Province? He believed there was hardly a man on the floor, who would get up and say, that he believed in his heart that the Government of this country would be a limited Monarchy: it would be Republican, most assuredly; nothing could prevent it. [Cheers.] If they inhabited an island in the midst of some immense sea, such a thing as a monarchy might be kept up; but adjoining the great American Union, the thing was impossible, it could not be done. [Cheers.] He therefore believed that the Government of this country must eventually become Republican; if therefore, they would found a good and lasting government for their country, they must base it on Republican principles, for none other could or would prevail in America. [Tremendous cheers, especially from the crowd of spectators in the gallery and below the bar.] They had seen, as he anticipated, from some of his friends, a great deal of that extreme admiration for existing institutions, which can see no fault, and that extreme sensibility which can bear no change, and they had heard a good deal of talk about "the ark of our constitution." But he [Mr. Gamble] would like to know where that ark was, and where the original principles of the constitution were to be found. The British Constitution, as had been truly remarked by Mr Mack, was called forth according to the circumstances of the times. This had been illustrated by Paley, when he said that it was not one great building put up at one time, but it had been constantly increasing; department after department had been added to it, not according to any fixed rule of architecture, but as was found to be convenient to the inhabitants, and he said that a building put up in that way, was one more adapted to the convenience of the inhabitants, than one constructed on architectural principles; and so with the constitution, it had altered from time to time to adapt itself to the circumstances of the day, and we must pursue the same course here; when we find our constitution won't work well, we must discover a remedy, and in this instance, he believed the remedy to be elective institutions; and if gentlemen would consider the subject, he was convinced they would arrive at the same conclusion [Cheers.]

Col. PLAYFAIR next addressed the Convention, much as follows; he said, Mr. Chairman, I cannot, after being a very attentive hearer, sit in my seat, without recording my vote against the Resolution, which has for its purpose an elective Legislative Council; I did think, sir, as it is an old saying that "'tis an ill wind that blows nobody good," that some good might arise out of the obnoxious Rebellion Losses Bill, (hear hear) and that in some sort of circumstances it was fortunate; not in the burning of the Parliament House, for I deplore any physical force demonstration, or any destruction of property, or breach of the peace; and no way fortunate in any insults offered to her Majesty's

Representative, for I do deeply deplore, in any part of the country, any indignity to the Representative of her Majesty. I reserve my opinion of the *man*, but I think that you and every gentleman here present, must know that opinion, or I should not be standing upon this floor, (cheers) ; I consider that the way good came to the Province was, that all the little evils and difficulties under which the Province suffers, formed little trains to the great train—the Rebellion Bill, which exploded and shook Canada from the centre to the circumference, and by that means roused the lethargic Conservatives to action, (hear, hear, hear) ; and by that shock, which is vibrating yet, this body has been called to assemble, or been moved to assemble together, and form themselves into an Association or League. Now, sir, I conceive that a league, covenant, or confederation, is a powerful moral engine, for good or evil, (hear, hear.) I consider that out of this League the very best of results may be drawn to Canada. I have said it was a powerful moral engine, and I think I can prove it. There was the Anti Corn Law League in England. I am a protectionist ; I am of the school of the late Lord Bentinck, (hear, hear) ; but I merely bring it forward to show that it was a powerful moral engine, and gentlemen are aware that there is another league formed and gaining strength in Britain, in which the agricultural and landed interests are concerned, and their motto—it makes my heart rejoice—is " Ships, Colonies and Commerce," (cheers) ; and sir, I will mention another league or confederacy, and that is the league the Barons entered into in the time of King John ; they stood before King John, and what did they obtain ? Why sir, they obtained the Magna Charta for England, and sir, the British American League have only to give a long pull, a strong pull, and a pull altogether, and they will obtain a Magna Charta for Canada. Well, it may be asked what is this magna charta ?— You have heard, sir, of Catholic emancipation, and of Negro emancipation : it will be Anglo-Saxon emancipation. From what,—from the British Crown ? No—no—no, sir, (cheers,) but from French fetters (cheers). It will put Messrs. Papineau and Lafontaine, and others, with Lower Canada, in the place where they ought to be ; they will be enabled, if they act wisely, judiciously and cautiously, to obtain a Federal Union. Then, sir, we can leave Lower Canada to herself ; she may then enjoy her feudal tenure, her feudal system, her *lods et vents* and her *cahots*. The eyes of the people will be opened, and they will come to the other portion of the confederacy for assistance in throwing off the fetters of their seigniors, (hear, hear.)— Sir, I am sorry to say that I cannot agree with the gentleman on the opposite side of the house. I will give him all credit for sincerity and loyalty ; for it is not because a man is disloyal, that he errs in judgment. Do I doubt the loyalty of General Packenham, when he commanded the troops at New Orleans, and met with such a defeat ? No sir, it was an error in judgment ; he did not know his enemy, or their

mode of fighting on that part of the continent. I do not wish to offend any gentleman, but I really think that an elective Legislative Council and an elective Governor is but one hair with annexation (laughter and cheers). I do not think you can split it ; and sir, I have heard a great deal about Downing Street, and I will own that there has been a great deal of error with respect to Canada, but at the same time we should remember with gratitude, what Britain had done for us, (cheers.) We are assembled here this evening as the *British* American League, but sir, if Great Britain had not put forth her fostering and powerful arm in 1837 and 8, to protect us, it is probable that instead of being a British American League, we should be all Republicans, and be assembled here for the purpose of sending delegates to Congress with remonstrances for some of our evils, (hear, hear.) Sir, if we had a Governor and Legislative Council, elected, it is probable that Great Britain would cast us off, and where is the man that would come out from under the paw of the British lion rampant, to fall into the fangs of the American eagle (great cheering). I would sooner be a dog and bay the moon, than such a Briton (renewed cheers and laughter). Then, sir, I cannot think of independence. I do not hesitate to make the assertion, and I would make it if Lord Wellington sat in that chair where you do, that Canada can never be independent. Canada, and I do not know what military men are present, is one of the hardest countries in the known world to defend ; Canada is what mathematicians give as the definition of a line ; Canada is " length without breath" (laughter.) It makes very little difference if you cut your throat, whether it is close to your chin or at your tongue, (laughter.) So it is with Canada. I may know something about it. I had the honor to defend Canada in the war of 1813, (cheers.) I crossed the Atlantic in 1812 with no friend but my sword, and I served during the whole of the war, on active service in Canada, and I know the difficulties she laboured under from her geographical position. I again assert that it is impossible to keep an army without an open rear, and as we lie alongside a powerful Republic, it is impossible to keep an open rear, without an immense force left behind. This was what caused a great deal of the trouble of Sir G. Prevost in 1813 ; he was obliged to leave his troops at this place and that place along the lines, or else he could not keep up the supplies. Cut off the supplies of an army, and it is like letting the blood out of your jugular vein. It is said by some that Canada can be independent. No man has a higher opinion of British valor than I have, but, as Wellington said on a certain occasion, " the greater the bravery, the greater the carnage"—and so would it be if we went to war with the United States ; I think, Sir, that the words of the Grecian poet would come to pass, when he says—

" Singly the Grecian heroes strove in vain—
New hosts opposed them, and they must be slain."

I believe that in the event of such a war Canada would do all that she can do, but in the words of the late Lord Castlereagh, speaking of the United States of America, he says : " Canada is alongside of a powerful republic," we can never therefore be independent. I am not one that would despair of all our wants being granted by the British Crown. (Hear, hear.) No, I do not despair, what was our distress in 1837 and 38, and did not Britain immediately pour forth her blood and her treasure, did not she spend three millions to put down the unnatural rebellion, and who can tell the amount of British blood which flowed on that occasion ? It only can be told in the annals of eternity. (Cries of question, question.) I can never go for this measure, no more than I can go forannexation. (Cheers.) I was at one time rather sorry that I came here, when I heard what extraordinary measures were to be brought forward, but now I am glad, because I will record my voice against those measures, and it will go back to those who sent me here. It has been said that Annexation is agitated through the length and breadth of the Province, but really when I awakened this morning I began to think that I could come from neither the length nor breadth of the Province, but I come from the Bathurst District, and there neither whigs nor tories are for Annexation, and if any individual were to go there to advocate Annexation, I really believe he would be rolled in the kennel. (Cheers and laughter.) If I did not record my vote against this measure I could not go back to those who sent me here, I could not look them in the face, nor could I look my family or my sons in the face, because I have always stated I considered it was leading us to fall into the hands of the great republic. I have said that I do not despair that we will have redress from the British Crown. I have already mentioned something of black emancipation ; did not Great Britain pay 20 millions to emancipate her negroes, and did not a poor Indian of the forest go home and take his wampum belt and present it to Her Majesty, filled with black beads and white, and what was the result ? The white beads were emblematical of the purity of their intentions, the black beads were emblematical of their grievances, and the poor Indian said our great mother the Queen directed the black beads to be taken out and the white to remain. (Cheers.) Now I think that if the League were to send home delegates and publications showing all our wants and grievances, that we should get what we want. (Hear, hear.) I cannot go for this resolution, because I am convinced it is taking us towards line 45, and I am proud of my birth as a Briton, proud of the exalted position which England holds in the scale of nations. (Cheers.) I am proud of her arts, her sciences, her literature, her commerce, her fleets, and her victorious armies, and again, I am proud because the sun never sets upon her territory, and I am prouder than all because the sun never sets upon her missionaries. (Cheers.) And Sir, let me remind you that it is righteousness which exalteth a nation, and if we are annexed or taken over by some other means, by some gilded pill, what will they annex us to ? It is said to the land of liberty—liberty to break the

sabbath—liberty to lynch—(cheers,)—liberty to buy and sell human flesh in the shambles.— (Cheers.) Why Sir, mark the noble sentiment of O'Connell, he would not even take their money, (loud cheers,) and our countrymen have now 56 ships at an annual expense of several millions on the coast of Africa, to put down the vile traffic in slavery. (Cries of question.) Sir, if I were to vote for that resolution, how could I meet my constituents or my family, and in the eternal world how could I meet my comrades who have fallen by my side in fighting to defend Canada from the United States. (Loud cheers.) How could I meet the spirit of my comrade Moodie ? How could I meet the spirit of my Colonel—Drummond ? With these remarks I shall record my vote against the motion.— (Great cheering.)

Mr. E. G. O'BRIEN rose amidst a perfect storm of cries of question and vote ; he was understood to say that he was not so much opposed to the resolution itself, which might under certain circumstances, if no better remedy could be obtained, improve the independence of the Legislative Council, but he regarded it as part of a whole—the stepping-stone to a measure of sweeping organic change in all our institutions, and as such he protested against it, and he thought it rather too bad that these revolutionary proposals should first come from the Conservatives, who had always professed to maintain British feelings and British institutions in the land.

Mr. DEEDES, amidst continued cries of question, stated that from all he had heard he was only confirmed in the opinion he entertained at Kingston, that it was neither necessary nor expedient to alter the present constitution of the Legislative Council.

Col. FRASER opposed the resolution, but from the position in which he stood, the purport of his remarks was not clearly understood at the reporter's table. He opposed this measure at Kingston, and he was opposed to it still, and so were his constituents in the Bathurst District ; from neither radical nor tory was a word to be heard about annexation or an elective Council He would oppose it as long as his name was Black Fraser. (Cheers and laughter.)

Capt. YOUNG, (Hillier,) had been sent to the Convention for the express purpose of opposing annexation or anything having a democratic tendency, and he would therefore vote against the motion.

Mr. WILSON believed that this was the only measure that would stop annexation ; he had been told by a friend who was a great annexationist, that if the League declared for the elective principle, he would denounce the annexation agitation and declare against it. In Quebec the annexation movement had been spreading so rapidly that he (Mr. W.) could not get together a meeting of his constituents before he left, because the office bearers had all become annexationists.

A vote was then taken on Mr. Murney's amendment, and it was lost by a large majority.

Mr. BENJAMIN then rose amidst shouts of

" vote" and "question," and moved the following resolution :—

That it is the opinion of the Convention that it is most essential to provide for the Independence of the Upper House or Legislative Council, and to guard against any possibility of an infringement of its privileges by the other branches of the Legislature, as well as to avoid the system of packing the Legislative Council by partizan appointments, which has a direct tendency to deprive that branch of the Legislature of that independence which the Constitutional Act contemplated it should enjoy, and that in order to remedy the defect in that body as at present constituted, it is advisable that the number of its members should be limited to, and constantly maintained at, half the number of the members of the Legislative Assembly.

He believed an elective Legislative Council would have a tendency to produce annexation ; it would bring in its train every other elective system this country could possibly have, he believed it would bring in its train an elective Governor, and thus sever the only remaining link which connects this colony with the parent state. He was quite willing to admit that the existing system of depriving the Legislative Council of its independence must be got rid of at once, and he believed it could be done by limiting the number of members. (Hear, hear.) It was true that the United States might not consent to take us, or to entertain the question of annexation while Great Britain refuses to assent to it, but the measure now proposed would lead to independence, and then the United States would say, now we will throw open our arms and receive you. He differed entirely from Mr. Gamble when he said that Canada must ultimately be Republican. England had reared colonies, he believed that England could rear nations and empires also. He would maintain the principles of monarchical institutions, because he believed them to be better than Republican. He did not think it followed that because we are alongside of a Republic, that we must adopt their doctrines and form of government. If we are monarchists at heart, our legislation should tend to establish a Monarchy. (Ironical cheers.) Gentlemen might laugh and sneer, but he could tell them that the feeling of the country was such, that he did not think they would ever be able to urge sufficient sophistry to change the present British feeling into Republicanism. He felt too, that in opposing this attempt to force on the country an elective Legislative Council, he was consulting not his own feelings only, but the feelings of those who sent him there. There were other reasons for which he would strongly and decidedly oppose the resolution ; he had as much courage, he believed, as the gentlemen opposite ; he dare do what most other men dare do—but he could not fly directly in the teeth of an oath he had taken—he had sworn steadily to maintain to the best of his ability, the connection between Great Britain and the British Colonies, and he would not abandon that obligation. (Cheers.)

Mr. A. J. McDonell seconded the amendment.

Mr. Gamble would like to know why the oath of allegiance had been introduced into the discussion ; the gentlemen acting with him regarded their oaths with as much sanctity as Mr. Benjamin, and they felt it more deeply, because

they desired to preserve this country to Great Britain, instead of forcing it from her. (Cheers.) He would not yield one inch to the gentleman in sincerity, or in regard for his oath ; he desired to act in these matters with the consent of Great Britain, and if Great Britain would discharge him from his oath of allegiance, he for one should hold that he was discharged from it. (Cheers.)

Mr. Aikman supported the amendment, as he was going to propose a similar one himself.

A division was then called for, when there appeared, for the amendment 34 ; against it 30 ; exclusive of the tellers.

The President then put the question " shall the original motion as amended be carried,"

Whereupon Mr. Gowan rose amidst cheers, and loud calls for a division, and great noise—he said, I think, Sir, that gentlemen will acquit me of any intention of obstructing the business of the Convention, for if there is one member more than another who has kept his place throughout the whole sitting, I may say that I have, nor have I obtruded my opinions on the Convention with regard to this question. Sir, the arguments urged here appear to me to be of a two-fold nature. First, it seems to be conceded on the part of gentlemen on both sides of the house, that if this question of an elective Legislative Council was consistent with the British Constitution, it would be an improvement, and it is opposed, solely, as I understand it, because they believe it to be inconsistent with the institutions under which they live.

Mr Rolland MacDonald, amidst loud cries of order, here interrupted the speaker to know, if his object was to gain time in order to procure votes, and if he had not sent out to bring in Delegates.

Mr. Gowan continued, Sir, if I had the object in view, which the learned gentleman imputes to me, I should not desire to carry out my intention better than by allowing him to interrupt me and put the questions he has done ; he has just taken the best means of delaying the business, and now if it will be any consolation to his heart, I beg to tell him that the first intimation of any intention of the kind has been from his lips. I never contemplated such a thing, although I confess that if I knew where there were any members escaping from their duties I should be most happy to send for them, as I think it desirable that there should be as full an expression of the opinions of the members on this question as possible. This measure is opposed because gentlemen say it is contrary to the British Constitution ; if I thought so I would oppose it, but can any gentleman stand up and tell me what part of the constitution under which we live, this motion is opposed to ? If any gentleman will show me that we are touching what is called " the ark of the constitution," then I will go with him. The time honoured constitution of which gentlemen talk, only dates its existence from 1841 : we first enjoyed a written constitution here when the Provinces were united—(no, no)—gentlemen say, " no, no," but I say that this time honoured and revered Constitution we have heard so much about, takes its date from

Lord Sydenham and the Government of 1841. (Hear, hear.) At that time all the gentlemen who held Seats in the Upper Branch of the Legislature of the country were deprived of their seats in the Legislature of the Province, and new members appointed. Was that no violation of the constitution? Did the honourable gentlemen opposite then say they would rather die than submit to Republicanism, or the tinkering of the Constitution? (Cheers.) Our Constitution, Sir, was then torn up by the King, Lords and Commons of England. Was that Republicanism? What I ask is our Constitution? A Constitution of eight years of age—a child, an infant—and yet we are told it is a time honoured constitution. Sir, one gentleman (Mr. A. J. Mc-Donell) asked us, if you elect your Legislative Council and Governor, where is the link that binds you to Great Britain? I asked the gentleman at the moment, where is the tie that unites Great Britain to the vast empire of India? The Governor General of India is a higher appointment than that of Canada, but by whom is he appointed? The Governor General of that immense empire is appointed by the Board of Control and vetoed by the East India Company. Then, Sir, when gentlemen tell me it is un-British, I tell them that it is British, and that it has been British as long as the name of Britain was known. (Cheers.) Mr. McKechnie has read to you the Charter granted by Charles II. to Connecticut. I could show you two other Charters granted to the old American Colonies, giving them unlimited power to elect their own Government, and which existed from the time of Charles II. down to the reign of George III., when they rebelled. We have shewn that it was British practice then, and we have proved by the case of India that it is British practice at the present day; how then can gentlemen tell us that it is un-British? what is the British Constitution?— Have gentlemen seen it or felt it? Is it not a constitution that adapts itself to the circumstances of the people, so as to promote the general prosperity and good Government? (Cheers.) Before closing I wish to call the attention of my learned friend opposite to the opinions of two of the great statesmen of the day, Sir Robert Peel and Lord Stanley. I would beg gentlemen to turn to the debate in the House of Commons on Mr Hawes's motion for curtailing the unnecessary expenses of the Imperial Government, in its colonies; turn to Sir Robert Peel's speech, and see his declaration there, that it was absurd to suppose that Colonists would continue to pay their Governors if they had no voice in the appointment of them (Cheers.) Then I would refer gentlemen to the close of Lord Stanley's speech on the Rebellion Losses Bill, where he stated that he feared the abuse of the prerogative in this case would drive the Colonists to seek for an elective Legislative Council to prevent the abuse of it. (Cheers.) And now we can bear the abuse heaped on us by gentlemen, as leaning towards annexation, as we are merely seeking the remedy which Lord Stanley foretold in his speech on the Rebellion Losses Bill. (Cheers.) I say nothing

about annexation, about loyalty or obligations, I should consider myself insulted to be spoken to on such subjects. I would point gentlemen to the history of my past life, they can read my principles there; (cheers,) where I have been ever found, there I am found to-day. I don't come here to vaunt my loyalty, the history of my life is the best index of the principles of my heart. (Cheers.)— In supporting this course I am actuated by a love for Britain; I believe that we cannot remain British unless we are as free as Britons.— (Cheers.) I believe that the freedom that we seek will tend to perpetuate the connection; the gentlemen who oppose us are making annexationists. I believe their course of policy is like the frightful policy that Lord North was pursuing when Lord Chatham foretold what would be the result of his policy. I believe the course the gentlemen opposite recommend to be similar—I sincerely hope it may never lead to similar results. (Loud cheers.)

The resolution as amended was then carried, and the Convention adjourned.

TUESDAY, Nov. 6, 10 A. M.

Mr. VANKOUGHNET moved a resolution for the appointment of a committee to meet at Halifax, to take further steps to carry out the union of the Provinces. [The resolution was the same as that which he afterwards moved and carried, and which will be found below, excepting that it contained a clause calling on the several local legislatures to take up the subject.]

It seemed to him necessary, after having adopted the report of the Committee of Conference, that they should take some action upon it. He was aware that there might be a difficulty in getting gentlemen to go to Halifax at this season of the year, but that could not be helped, they should at all events authorise them to go, in case any gentlemen should be willing to go. He also thought it necessary that the principle which Mr. Gamble stated was embraced in his (Mr. G.'s) third resolution should be carried out, viz., that the local Legislatures should take up the subject, although he had objected to the mode in which Mr. Gamble proposed to carry it out.

Mr. DIXON objected to the resolution, as it had been agreed by his amendment that it was necessary to lay down the principles on which the union could take place, before consulting the people or the Legislature. His only object was to facilitate business and bring things to a focus, and if the Convention was satisfied that Mr. Vankoughnet's resolution would effect that object better than his, he would withdraw it.

Mr. VANKOUGHNET withdrew his resolution rather than let it interfere with Mr. Dixon's.

A long and uninteresting discussion on a point of order then ensued, which ended in Mr. Dixon reading the sketch of a Constitution that he had drawn up, and laying it on the table for the consideration of the members. [The substance of this sketch has been given before.]

Mr. STRACHAN (Goderich) . likewise laid on the table the following sketch, embodying his views of the terms on which the proposed union could take place :—

1st. That the Canadas, with New Brunswick, Nova Scotia, Prince Edward's Island, and Newfoundland, be joined in one Federal Union under the name of " British North America."

2nd. The Queen's title to be then, Queen of the United Kingdom of Great Britain, Ireland and British North America—British North America to have a Secretary and office in Downing Street to itself, and to be governed by a Viceroy with a Federal Legislature.

3rd. Each Province to have a separate Government for the management of local matters, the Legislative Council of each Province to be Elective, by a Special Election, with a higher qualification, both on the part of the Electors and Elected, than is required in the Provincial Assembly.

4th. The Legislative powers to be granted to the Federal Government, shall be vested in a General Assembly or Parliament, consisting of the Governor-General or Viceroy, a Legislative Council and House of Assembly. Such General Assembly or Parliament, to continue six years from the day of returning the writs for choosing the same, and no longer, subject nevertheless to be sooner prorogued or dissolved, by the Governor General or Viceroy.

5th. The Legislative Council shall be composed of six members from each Province, to be chosen by the Governor, Lieutenant Governor, or person administering the government of the several Colonies, from their respective Legislative Councils, or of persons selected by the Crown from the most prominent men in the respective Provinces, or of persons elected by the Legislatures themselves, from among their own number; the period of their service to be six years, one-third to retire every second year.

6th. The House of Assembly shall be composed of — members, chosen by the Provincial Assemblies from among their own number, or by a special election, but with a higher qualification, both on the part of the electors and elected, than is required in the Provincial Assemblies.

7th. That a deputation of three members from the Legislative Council, selected by the Governor General from that body, or three out of six proposed by the Legislative Council for his choice, and six chosen by the House of Assembly from among its own members, have seats in the House of Commons.

8th. This General Legislature or Parliament shall have power—

" 1st. To lay on and collect taxes, duties and imposts—the same to be uniform throughout the Union.

2nd. To assume and pay the debts of the several Provinces, and provide for the peace and welfare of the Union.

3rd. To establish uniform Commercial Regulations between the different Provinces, and between them and Foreign Countries, provided the same be not repugnant to the Laws of the United Kingdom.

4th. To determine all disputes that may arise between the Provinces.

5th. To regulate the Navigation of Rivers and Lakes, common to two or more Provinces, or common to any Province or Provinces and a Foreign Power.

6th. To open internal communication for the general advantage, such as roads, canals, railroads, steam navigation, &c.

7th. To establish and regulate the Post Office and Post Roads, within the Union.

8th. To adopt and establish an uniform system of Militia Laws, and to provide for calling forth the Militia—to execute the laws, to suppress insurrection and repel invasion."

9th. All bills for raising revenue, shall originate in the House of Assembly, but the Legislative Council may propose or concur with amendments, as in other bills.

10th. There shall be a Supreme Court to take cognizance of causes, respecting the breach of the Union laws, and questions between inhabitants of the different Provinces, and between them and foreigners.

11th. This tribunal shall likewise be a Court of Appeal in certain cases from the Provincial Courts, and its decision shall be final. All proceedings to be in the English language, not only in the Supreme Court, but in all the interior Courts of the Colonies.

12th. Persons charged in any Province with treason, felony or other crime, who shall flee from justice, and be found in any of the other Provinces of the Union, shall, on demand of the Executive authority of the Colony from which they fled, be delivered up to be removed into the Province having jurisdiction of the crime:

13th. The portion of the Revenue at the disposal of the general Legislature for public purposes, shall be the surplus after defraying the expenses of the Civil Government of the respective Provinces, which shall be settled by general enactment.

14th. Several other powers, such as impeachment, regulation, and protection of the fisheries, &c. &c. &c., might be conferred on the supreme Legislature.

Mr. STRACHAN accompanied his sketch with the following remarks :—The advantages resulting from a general Union, possessing the free and liberal constitution which I have briefly sketched, are many and important. I shall mention a few of the most obvious. I conceive such a Union would connect the different Provinces so intimately, as must insure, in a little time, a community of feeling as well as interest, and thus carry along with it the popular voice. I conceive further, that the number of members being comparatively few and intelligent, would be more easily guided to right principles, and being composed of the most influential men from all the colonies, a more correct policy would be adopted in their proceedings, than can be expected from the Provincial Legislatures. Again, I feel that a seat in the Legislative Council or Assembly would become a great and honourable object of ambition, and success would produce nearly the same effect on aspiring young men, as a title in Great Britain.. We must all see at a glance, that this superior Legislature would be naturally attached to the Parent State, as a link of connection; and, being composed of the most eminent men of all the colonies, their good sense would induce them to value. this advantage, as the palladium of their safety and civil rights—the source of their prosperity and future prospects. Moreover, the deputation to the House of Commons would identify the Union with the Parent State, and ensure its adherence, from the conviction that such an intimate connection was inseparable from a community of interests. Further, this Union, by consolidating the resources of the Provinces, and directing them with unity of design, would become a complete barrier to encroachments from the United States; a new, and inexhaustible field of laudable ambition for our youth, much beyond any thing now before them, would be opened. Hence a love of their country would be strengthened, and the united Provinces, from their rapid increase of population, and their attachment to British institutions, would daily become more formidable in war and respectable in peace. In regard to the Lower portion of the Province of Canada, the feelings and apprehensions, which at present distract its peace, would gradually subside without any disagreeable struggle.— The Canadian character would, by degrees, sink into the English without irritation, for they could never expect to acquire a paramount influence in a Legislature, of which they were only a component part; and, as the language of the Parent State would be the language of the superior Legislature in its proceedings, of the Courts of Justice, and all other public business, every man wishing to attain eminence must study to acquire it. Again, the great ease with which the colonies would be governed, is not the least advantage,—all communications of importance would be from one instead of six governments; and the little details at present so perplexing, would find their solution from the Superior Government. The colonies are at present very liable to become estranged from each other, and to adopt different views respecting their own interests and their communications with foreign States. The Union would cure these evils by preserving inviolable the interests of each, and adopting one uniform rule for all, in their intercourse with foreign powers and with one another. Moreover, the connection between the British North American colonies and the West Indies, would soon become more intimate,—commercial intercourse would no longer be confined to one Province, but would range through the whole. Halifax in Nova Scotia, St. Johns and St. Andrews in New Brunswick, instead of being almost unknown to the Canadas, might soon become places of general depot, and the ports at which Canadians might often embark for England. Canals, roads, railways, and steam navigation, would, under a strong and united government, soon be set agoing—capitalists would be attracted—improvements urged and carried out—the fisheries on the coast would be "encouraged, and enterprize promoted, and the resources of the different Provinces rendered a kind of common stock, by which they would become more intimately acquainted, and by which a most important and valuable internal commerce among themselves would be produced. The fisheries alone present an inexhaustible mine of wealth and strength. Indeed, I think the present ill-judged commercial policy now adopted by the Mother Country, renders a general Union of the Provinces most desirable, if not absolutely necessary for their own protection and prosperity. The colonies, thus united, would in time become one of the greatest nations in the world. They enfilade in the interior of the country the greater portion of the United States, and at the same time possess a seaboard more extensive than any other nation of the world. Hence they possess the elements of immense power, from the products of their land, their convenient ports, and the fisheries upon their shores, which are mines infinitely superior to those of Peru or California. Again, another advantage of infinite importance, would be the greater facility with which the moral and religious improvement of the population might be conducted, and institutions established similar to those in the parent state, by which they would learn to distinguish between liberty and licentiousness, and between social tranquillity and anarchy (cheers). With these remarks, I offer to the Convention the synopsis of a constitution, which I have brought forward. I feel deeply interested in this subject, and I think, from the way in which we have been going on for some time past, that unless some strong measures be adopted, Canada will be lost to Great Britain. I have taken no part in the discussions since I came into this Convention, because I felt that there was no necessity for me to urge my views, solitary and alone, which I knew others were determined to oppose under any circumstances. I was sorry at some of the opinions I have heard expressed, but I am glad that matters have been so arranged that we can work harmoniously together; and I trust that when we break up, we shall break up with some strong and energetic remedy for the evils of the country (cheers).

After considerable discussion as to the order of business,

Mr. MILLER rose and said, that he should now bring up the resolution of which he gave notice on Saturday evening, relative to the engrossing question lately agitating the Province—the question of annexation. He brought the resolution forward on the present occasion from the fact, that if there had been one there had been twenty members of the Convention who desired that the question should not be brought up, and that no public expression shoud be given by the Convention on the question of annexation; and who seemed desirous to allow the impression to go forth to the country, that the Convention allowed it to pass by silently; and the conclusion naturally would be, that the majority of the

present annexation party were formerly supporters of the Conservative party, and that the Convention, if not actually in favour of annexation,
were at all events not strenuously opposed to it,
which would operate most materially against the
influence of the Convention and against the interests of that portion of the people whom they
represented. He had drawn up the resolution
with great care, so as not to irritate or annoy
any who might be in favour of a contrary course,
or in any way to infringe on that cordial feeling
which ought to exist. He moved—

" That it is a matter of regret to this Convention,
that the subject of a separation of this Colony from the
Mother Country, and Annexation to the United States
of America, has been openly advocated by a portion of
the press, and inhabitants of this Province ; and this
Convention unhesitatingly records its entire disapprobation of this course, and calls upon all well-wishers of
their country to discountenance it by every means in
their power."

In supporting the resolution he should merely
refer to one or two of the arguments used by
those who favoured annexation, and then leave
the question in the hands of those with more experience and much better able to discuss it than
he was. The times in which we live would seem
to afford an excuse for almost any revolutionary
scheme which may be set on foot, and are prolific
of events which set all theory and all well settled
opinions at defiance ; but among all the startling
movements which had been made, he believed
there were none which possessed the peculiar and
characteristic feature of our Canadian revolutionary scheme, its supporters disavowing any
intention of a forcible demonstration, whilst at
the same time it must be evident to them, and to
every one else, that there is not the remotest
chance of a peaceable consummation of their
wishes ; they are dissolving the bands of
society and revolutionizing the country, not
for the purpose of maintaining the great
principles of civil and religious liberty, but
for the purpose of trafficking in human
rights and in mercantile interests for the
mere chance of commercial advantages. The
great argument on which the Annexationists
found their opinion, is that of interest ; our
geographical position, our contiguity to the
United States, and the circumstances which at
present regulate commercial intercourse between us and the United States, and between us
and the Mother Country, are the arguments on
which they propose to tear us from the Mother
Country and precipitate us into the arms of a rival nation. It is said that Great Britain has deprived us of protection in her markets, that she
has put us on the same footing with foreign nations, and thereby subjected us to the severest
competition ; and that the free trade policy of
England and the want of reciprocity with the
United States, has placed the Canadian farmer
in a disadvantageous position, as he is unable to
compete with the American ; and it is confident-
ly stated as a remedy for this evil, that Annexation to the United States would give us the advantage of the American market, and place us
in the same advantageous position with our
neighbours on the other side of the line. This

he believed was the great argument advanced by
the Annexationists, and if they could throw a
suspicion on the propriety or correctness of the
conclusions which were deduced from these
facts, the whole scheme must fall to the ground.
He should not attempt to point to statistical
details or bring up any facts to disprove that
position ; he should leave that to those whose
profession and calling would enable them to do
so better, but he should merely devote himself to
one point—why is it that the Canadian farmer
has not access to the American market ? It is
because you find that there is a duty of 20 per
cent. against him, and why is this duty imposed ?
It is because the American agriculturist has applied to the American Government for protection
against competition from our farmers. It is because Canada is capable of becoming one of the
greatest wheat-growing countries in the world,
and because if we were allowed even for a few
years to have free access to the American market, the immense and inexhaustible resources of
our country would be developed to such an extent, that the produce sent from Canada would
almost swamp the American market. It is for
this reason that a duty of 20 per cent is imposed
by the Americans against Canadian wheat. But
supposing the annexation movement consum-
mated, what then would be the result ? They
would find that so soon as that barrier was
removed between our produce and the American market, those resources of our country
would be drawn out and developed, every
energy of the country would be drawn out, and
the accumulation of produce to which he had adverted would be the consequence, and if there be
any truth in the well established principle of
political economy, that the demand and supply
will regulate the price of the commodity, if the
experience of every day be correct, which teaches
us that the fluctuations of commerce are dependent on a thousand contingencies, so sure as we
are annexed to the United States we would be
subjected to all the contingencies which demand
and supply and the fluctuations of commerce
will effect in the country. Then there is the
American tariff, to which we would then be subjected, the slightest change in which might sweep
away at one stroke the interests of the agricultu-
rists, and subject them to the interests of the
growers of cotton or tobacco, or the sugar manufacturers, or sacrifice them to the interests of the
mercantile community, and any or all must be subservient to the caprices of party. Where then is
the argument of the annexationists, that annexation would be a present benefit or a present re-
lief to our commercial difficulties ? Another argument adduced by the annexationists, and one
that had had an important effect in the spread of
the movement, was, that England desires to cast
us off, that she is tired of us, and that the moment the colonists express a wish to separate, she
would let us go, and in fact be glad to get rid of
us. Since this had become an important argument in the annexation movement, it was time
to ascertain on what foundation it rests. Let
those who support the annexation movement,
state on what authority they found that argu-

ment. Is it on any message from either House or any other public document or official despatch? No, there was no such document, everything of the kind which has emanated from any British authority is marked by no other than kind and anxious regard for the welfare of these colonies and the continuation of their connection with the mother country; to find such sentiments and feelings as those referred to, they must look to the language of the Manchester Chartists or the no less dangerous sentiments of the radical party. The opinions of Lords Brougham, Stanley, and even Lord John Russell, as expressed in public speeches on recent occasions, had been referred to by the annexationists in support of this argument; but he would ask under what circumstances were those speeches made, and those sentiments delivered? It was at a time when this country was distracted from one end to the other by rebellion, and when England was obliged for the maintenance of her authority and government here, to enforce the dreadful expiation of blood for blood; it was when her hands were embrued in the blood of her own subjects, that these statesmen stood forward as the friends of humanity, and said that they would infinitely prefer, if it was the desire of these colonies to separate from the mother country, to dissolve the connection rather than these unnatural and inhuman circumstances should continue. It was at such a time, when patriotism and loyalty to their country were struggling against the vilest feelings of humanity, that these sentiments were uttered. What advantage therefore the annexationists could derive from that argument he was at a loss to imagine; and so at the time of the recent occurrences in Montreal, similar sentiments were expressed under the influence of similar feelings, as those occurrences were not properly understood by the British government. The third argument advanced, and not only by the annexation party, but he was sorry to say by a portion of the Conservative party also, is that it is a mere question of time, that we must sooner or later go over to the United States, and that therefore the sooner we begin to prepare the way the better. He considered that any Conservative who made use of that argument did so without due reflection on the causes that would lead to a consummation of that kind, and without any regard to the consequences of making use of such expressions He would admit that time was necessary to develope the abuses and errors in the Government of this country, that might be prejudicial to its interests, but time would likewise develope and strengthen our feelings of attachment and regard to the mother country, if the principles and influences which operate in forming the national feeling and national prejudices are in the first instance favourable to them, and he asserted that those causes and influences were at work in this Colony. When these Colonies were peopled by refugees from rebellious and revolutionary states, when they were afterwards taken under the fostering care and protection of the British Government, until from being an insignificant place of refuge they became the most important Colony of the empire; when these things were brought about, a feeling of loyalty was fixed and firmly planted in the breasts of the people of this country, which no circumstances can eradicate Look how this feeling was displayed in 1812, when the inhabitants of this Colony showed their devotion to the interests of the mother country, and their determination to adhere to the connection, and transmit the same feeling to their posterity; and nearly a quarter of a century later, when the rebellion broke out and there was scarcely a soldier to be found in Upper Canada, the same feeling evinced itself, and the same unanimity was exhibited in support of the connection with the mother country at all hazards and under all circumstances; this feeling of loyalty and affection may be crushed and broken down under the influence of continued insult and injury, but it can never be eradicated from our minds. He would not detain them further than merely to refer to the assertion in the Montreal Manifesto, that they only desire *peaceable* separation from the mother country; he considered this a kind of spurious loyalty—a Judas loyalty which proffers the kiss of affection to the Sovereign as the emblem of its treason, and if there was one thing in that Manifesto which more than another deserved disapprobation, it was the paltry attempt to palliate the insult offered to every loyal mind by connecting words of peace, and consideration for the wishes of our Queen and the connection with the mother country, with sentiments of disloyalty to that Queen and her Government. He had brought forward this subject of annexation not with a view of creating division, but in order that the Convention, as the representatives of the Conservative party, might stamp it with their disapprobation, and urge the members of their party throughout the Province to discountenance it by all the means in their power. (Loud cries of question and vote.)

Mr. ROLLAND MCDONALD rose for the purpose of seconding the motion, amidst loud shouts of "question." When order was restored, he said, Those gentlemen are only exposing their ignorance of my character, if they think they will put me down. In rising to second the resolution, I would merely avail myself of the right which has been conceded to every individual who has either moved or seconded a resolution, to say a few words. Gentlemen need not be too thin-skinned. I shall not be too hard on those suspected of Annexation leanings; for I maintain that there is not an individual in this assembly at this moment prepared to go for annexation, although some may be suspected of having leanings that way. But they need not be so thin-skinned; I am very mild, and shall direct all I have to say, against those who have come out in favour of annexation. Neither do I intend that any of my remarks shall apply to those worthy individuals who have signed the Montreal manifesto. There are men who have put their names to that document, as loyal, as truly British, as any man on the floor of this house; many of those individuals have signed that document in a moment of pique—many in order to compel Great Britain to take notice of our position. I know that there are men who have signed their names to that manifesto, who would spill their hearts' best blood to keep up British connection and British sway (cheers); therefore I would be the last man to say a word against those individuals. I desire to reclaim them by giving them hope for the country, and showing them a way to get out of their declarations. I do not wish to drive these people by despair into the position, that they must stand or fall by that which they have put their names to. It has been well understood during the whole of this convention, that I was most desirous of having the matter brought up for consideration and the decision of the meeting; because I felt that it was impossible for a body like this, assembled ostensibly for the purpose of taking into consideration the political state of the country, to separate without giving their opinion one way or the other, on the great question which we are told now agitates the public mind from one end of the province to the other; and when members, with the very best intentions, brought forward measures such as the introduction of the elective principle into institutions in which it has never appeared before, I felt that it became imperatively necessary for us to say that, notwithstanding we have introduced these propositions, still we are the same now as we have ever been. It has been said by some gentlemen to-day, that they are still of the same opinion that they were last evening, with respect to elective institutions. I will state a fact to them, which will, I think, induce many of them to pause in the career they have entered on. Every individual who has spoken in favour of these institutions, has stated that he is in favour of them for the purpose of strengthening the tie that binds us to the mother country. Now, when I tell them this fact, they may well pause and consider whether they are on that track which will lead to a further cementing of that connection. Sir, I spoke this morning to a friend of mine, who is an annexationist; and knowing him to be one, I said, "Now, my friend ———, what is your honest opinion on this subject?—I know you to be an annexationist—what is your opinion of our proceedings, especially of the resolutions brought in by Mr. Wilson—is the course we are pursuing tending to keep up the connection with Great Britain, or to separation?" He replied honestly, "The men bringing forward these resolutions may not mean it, but they are playing the very game of the annexationists; I would not desire them to do anything better, as nothing would hurry annexation so surely as the measures they bring forward."

A DELEGATE. Was that gentleman one who believes in annexation as a remedy under all circumstances, or one who regards annexation as a last resource?

Mr. McDONALD. That is certainly a question which is fairly to be considered. He is an individual who is for annexation under any circumstances. Now, if these gentlemen really and sincerely believe, as they say, that the introduction of the elective principle is the only thing to prevent annexation, I will ask them to consider whether it is not a most suspicious and strange circumstance, that upon all the measures which Mr. Wilson has brought forward to strengthen our connection with Great Britain, he has got the votes of every man suspected of annexation tendencies? If those in favour of annexation felt that the view taken by Mr. Wilson is correct, and that he is knocking the ground from under them—taking away the platform on which we are standing, would not they have opposed the resolutions?—and is not the fact of their voting for the resolutions enough to induce those persons who honestly think they are doing right, to pause and say, "After all, I believe I am on a dangerous course; if these resolutions are going to cement the connection with the mother country, it is a very strange thing they get the vote of every gentleman having annexation tendencies"? When I come by and by to answer the arguments of the annexationists, and say, "You annexationists," mind I don't mean anybody in this assembly, but some imaginary annexationists, beyond the window there (pointing towards Messrs. Wilson and Gamble). Now, sir, with respect to the question of annexation, I'll tell you what appears to me to be the most important point at this moment. We have an election going to take place in the Third Riding of this county, and I do think it one of the most important things, that in the very first election in which annexation or anti-annexation comes up, that the annexation candidate should be rejected (hear, hear). Now, here is a point on which I want to say a word or two to the present administration. I stated on a former occasion, that if I felt they were sincere; that if I felt that Messrs. Cameron, Hincks and Baldwin were sincere in their desire to continue and perpetuate British connection, and not to sell us to a foreign country; if I felt that, I have said, and I repeat it, I would vote for those men, though I have no confidence in them, against my own brother, if that brother was an annexationist (hear, hear). But, sir, it is important for the ministry, if they desire to have the people of this country believe they are in earnest, to bring forward a candidate for the purpose of opposing Mr. Perry; and if they do not do so, the people of the country will take leave to doubt their professions on this subject. (A VOICE. They have done so.) I am delighted to hear it; and if I had a vote in that county, and had to walk a hundred miles—though I am not fond of walking—I would do it to record my vote against Mr. Perry, and for any other candidate, no matter if he be the greatest radical. I am glad to hear that they have done so, and I would say that that very declaration of Mr. Baldwin has tended in a great measure to soften my feelings towards that individual. If Mr. Montgomery, or Mr. Charles Durand, or any one else comes to me and tells me that he rebelled in 1837, because he had not his rights as a British subject, which have been conceded to him since, and that he can now gird on his sword to defend the rights he has acquired under Great Britain; that man I would give my hand to and respect him as a brother, and throw the old terms of conservative and reformer to the winds (hear, hear). Now, sir, I would like to make one or two remarks with respect to an individual just before me. Mr. Gamble made use of an expression which I think he must be sorry for; he said he did not come here to speak about loyalty *and that sort of thing.* Now, I am sorry that in a British assembly loyalty should be spoken of in this way. He also spoke about "spaniel loyalty," and about his loyalty "oozing out, like Bob Acres' courage, at his fingers' ends." Well, he may have no loyalty towards Great Britain, but there is a loyalty of another kind—although mind I don't say that any individual here has that kind of loyalty: did any of you ever hear of Punch's new discovery, the Flourometer (laughter); Punch has it something in this way—

" Flour 33s. per barrel—loyalty up.

Flour 26s. per barrel—cloudy.

Flour 22s. per barrel—down to annexation."

(Cheers and laughter.)

Now Sir, I would say a word or two with respect to the arguments of the annexationists, of whom, as I said before, there are none in this room. One of their arguments is about the better price of wheat. Well that was sufficiently replied to by Mr. Miller, I won't say a word about that. Another argument is that the price of land would be higher. Do they mean wild land ? Because we all know wild land is cheaper in the U. S. What land do they mean ? Is it land in this city? I can tell them there is land in this city, and in Hamilton, and St. Catherines too, which sells at a higher price per foot, than in cities of larger growth in the U. S. They tell us also that the country is more prosperous, that is the main argument. Now, why is the country more prosperous ? Because there is a fictitious prosperity given to our neighbors through the means of money which they have borrowed from England, which I believe they will never repay. There is also another reason, there is not a petty mill in the U. S., there is not a blacksmith's shop, there is not a tavern and ten-pin-alley but what sports a bank ! (Cheers and laughter.) That, Sir, is the thing that satisfies me, that their prosperity is not based on a solid foundation, in fact, I consider the prosperity of the U. S. like their institutions, a delusion. (Ironical cheers.) It is a stupendous fraud. (Ironical cheers.) I think, Sir, that like the fruit on the banks of the Dead Sea, it seems to be all fair without to the eye, but it is all bitterness and ashes within. (Cheers.) Now we have been told that we have got to join the United States, because England has not given us what we want. Is there anything that we have ever asked her that she has refused ?— What did we ask her ? Who were the people in this country who asked for free trade ? It was the Montreal people who said, we want free trade and no favour. England gave it them, and what do they want next ? The abrogation of the Navigation Laws, and England gave that up too What else have we asked for ? The Reformers asked for Responsible Government. England gave it to them ; she has allowed us in point of fact to be almost completely independent : she has given us money for canals; lent us her credit;

done all that the parent can do for the child, and yet because she would not go further and interfere in the Rebellion Losses Bill, we that have been called " loyal' *par excellence,* are going to annex ourselves. (Cheers in the gallery.) Now look at the inconsistency of the thing. We have been saying that England should leave us to ourselves, and yet what brought us together ?— Because England refused to interfere in the Indemnity Bill, and therefore we have got to rebel, although we have always said, and said it in this Convention, that we do not want her to interfere at all ! It is just the inconsistency people fall into who are determined to carry out some particular views of their own at the moment.— Now let us look what we shall give up, provided we should have annexation ? What have we always been asking for ? We have been asking for the perfect control of our public lands, we would not allow Great Britain or the Sovereign of Great Britain, to whom we have sworn allegiance, to have the control of the public lands. But what are the Annexationists going to do ? They are willing, almost the moment we have got the control of these public lands, to hand them over to the United States ! Is it not most singular inconsistency ? Well, Sir, there is our Customs revenue. It was a long time before we had the control of our own affairs in that matter. We have hardly got that control when we are prepared to quarrel with the Mother Country, and turn over that control to the people at Washington. Then there is the matter of the Post Office, we have always more or less been harping on that subject; we have asked Great Britain over and over again to give us the complete controul of our Post Office ; and above all, the Post Master General, and that he should not pocket 7 or 8,000 pounds a year from the people of this colony; and just at the moment that Great Britain has conceded that—at that very moment we say, we dont want Great Britain to have the controul of the Post Office, but we want it to go to Washington ! Did you ever know of such inconsistency? Well then, look at the immense amount of money spent by the troops in this country, hard Mexican dollars, we are also willing to give up all that.— Look at the money laid out by Great Britain in fortifications ; we say we dont want that either, we are too rich already. But after giving all this up, we reserve to ourselves the right of taxing ourselves directly to carry on our Government. We give up our revenue, our public lands, the Post Office ; we say, we wont have any of these things, we will be directly taxed to support our Government ; the taxes will then be double, treble and quadruple what they are now. Now sir, having shortly alluded to the advantages and disadvantages, I would ask another question —I am speaking of course to the imaginary annexationists on the other side of the house— Are you sure that the United States will have anything to do with you ? you go about with your loyalty in your hands and are willing to annex yourselves ; look at the tone of contempt in which you are spoken of by the people of the United States. Are you sure that the people of the United States will have anything to do with you? I am one of those who think that the annexation of Upper Canada would be one of the worst things that could happen to the United States—it would break up the union; unless they took Cuba from Spain, the thing could not be entertained at all. I will read, gentlemen, what the American newspapers say of us—they say: "now we can assure our Canadian contemporary, that he is entirely mistaken in the conclusion at which he has arrived with regard to receiving sympathy in the United States. It is very certain that the United States will never permit the Canadians to annex themselves to this Republic under any circumstances whatever; but while we assert this, we are willing on the other hand to say, that if the Canadians will at some future time procure the consent of Great Britain to be annexed to the United States, we will, when this consent shall have been obtained and on their solicitation." You have to go with your hat in your hand and ask to be admitted; knock humbly at the door, perhaps more than once, and on your solicitation you may get in; they'll not have you then, but take the matter into their serious consideration, just as Lord Elgin did our petitions on the Rebellion Losses Bill, (hear, hear and laughter,) "and if we can adjust some preliminary arrrangements concerning our domestic relations"—that's slavery "satisfactorily to the varied interests in this country, we would allow them to come in and partake of the great political blessings"—Lynch law, universal suffrage, vote by ballot, annual congress, and all those other blessings "that the United States holds out to an admiring world, and which we in the United States enjoy." Well, supposing that you have got into the Union, then comes the question whether Great Britain dare give you up. This matter has been very ably spoken of by Mr. Wilson. He said Great Britain will not give us up, but I go further than he did, and say that Great Britain dare not give us up—dare not consent to lose one of her first colonies, and by that means commence a retrograde movement that would lead to her dissolution, or at all events to her becoming some third, fourth or fifth power in the world—the British Minister that would dare bring into the House of Commons such a proposition, would be impeached, and his head would be deservedly laid low on the block: no statesman dare propose it, and I'll tell you what more—I am one of those who think that so long as there is any considerable portion of the people of this Province to tell you they won't be annexed—to tell you, *leges Angliæ nolumus mutari,* so long will Great Britain be in honour bound to protect those that desire to remain attached to her, and that you cannot get annexation even if you had the majority of the people in your favour. It would be part and parcel of the honour of Great Britain to protect those that desired to remain attached to her, and Great Britain has never been found wanting when called upon by the meanest of her subjects for protection. Then gentlemen, what would you do about your debt, you would have to pay a fair portion of the debt of the United States, and what would

you do about your own debt? These things, so important in my view, are so trifling to the annexationists that they jump them over. Now I would say a word about the annexation newspapers started in this country. I will do what I can to give the Government and people of this country good information concerning them, though I may ensure myself a pretty good share of abuse. I am currently informed that the two annexation newspapers that have been brought forward in this country, in Montreal and Toronto, are supported by foreign gold. (Ironical cheers.) I tell you sir, that the story goes, that some of the money that was subscribed by the sympathisers in the United States for the Rebellion in Ireland, that ended in the little scrimmage in Mrs. McCormack's cabbage garden, was unfortunately not required because the thing was put down before they had time to send over the money; this money remained in the hands of the Irish Directory in New York, it was intended to bring about a repeal of the union between Great Britain and Ireland, and thereby to lessen that great kingdom in the eyes of the world. What did these people do next? they said the best thing they could do was to send that money to Canada. I have it on undoubted authority, that that money has gone to support a paper called the *Independent.* That is the way the story goes. I hope there is no truth in it. The owner of that paper was considered good security, and the money was handed to him on the understanding that it would be applied for a particular purpose. Mr. Sidney Bellingham, of Montreal, was not considered good security. The very individual in Montreal who applied to the Irish Directory for the money, and who was obliged to give security for Mr. Bellingham told it in Montreal, he belongs to a firm there, and the money was handed over to him and he now pays it as they go along. (Hear, hear) It may not be true, but I am satisfied that these papers could not be well supported in this country, and nothing is more natural than to suppose that they are supported by foreign gold. (Hear, hear.) It has been said that the feeling for annexation is growing in this country—that the people are ripening for it. What did Col. Playfair tell us the other night in his truly patriotic speech? what did Black Fraser tell us also? That with respect to annexation and elective institutions, such a thing was never heard of in the Bathurst District, where the people are nearly all Reformers; and I'll tell you what is more, you are talking about your elective institutions; they are not asked for by the people. There is not a man here can tell me that he was instructed by his constituents to ask for elective institutions. (Question, question.) Now you speak about annexation. I shall show you what the feeling is; you say the feeling of annexation is growing in the country, I'll show you what the feeling is. There was a meeting at Grimsby the other day—as fine a lot of fellows as any in the country; these persons held a meeting, and what are the sentiments they have recorded. I'll ask my friend Mr. Miller to read them to you while I recover my voice.

Mr. MILLER rose to read the resolutions, but was met by vociferous shouts of " spoke," so that he was compelled to hand the paper, the Niagara *Chronicle*, to Mr. Dixon, who read as follows :—

BRITISH AMERICAN LEAGUE.

At a meeting of the Grimsby Branch of the British American League, held on the 24th of October, 1849, the following resolution was adopted :—

WHEREAS a document has been put forth in the City of Montreal which contains treasonable and seditious assertions of the expediency of Canadians repudiating their allegiance as British subjects, and seeking admission into the Republic of the United States of America, and

WHEREAS it is attempted to be shown that the grievances under which her Majesty's most loyal and tried Canadian subjects lately laboured are a sufficient excuse for any endeavours to sever the tie which binds Canadians to their fatherland, and

WHEREAS the proposition to abjure an allegiance endeared as is that which every Canadian owes by the ties of soil, of blood, and a common liberty, can only be entertained by the unprincipled, the sordid, and the selfish,

Therefore, be it resolved, That instructions be given to the Representatives of this branch of the British American League to express their abhorrence of the principles enunciated in the document put forth in Montreal, already adverted to, and to assure the members of the General Convention, that the members of this branch are fully determined, by the help of God, by whom " nations and empires rise and fall, flourish and decay," to tread in the paths of their forefathers, and to stand by the flag which has 'braved the battle and the breeze' so long as it shall please Him to permit them to exist. That they utterly repudiated, as offensive to God and man, the specious fallacy that a man is justified from capricious or any other motives in abjuring his country and alienating the strength of his right arm from the defence of his native land, or any part of the glorious and mighty empire of which it is their privilege to form a part.

> J. B. PETIT, *Vice Prest.*
> Chairman.

E. T. P. GURNEY, *Sec'y.*

Mr. McDONALD then rose to go on with his speech, but was met by loud cries of " question" and " spoke," and much laughter.

Mr. E. G. O'BRIEN rose to order. Did gentlemen think the question of annexation such a paltry one, that we must treat the question in this way? One gentleman in particular, Mr. Gamble,—

MR. GAMBLE here rose to order. If the gentleman made these personal observations, he should have to answer them. All he desired was, that the arguments of the annexationists should be met by argument, and not by a mere matter of feeling On behalf of the gentlemen near him, he disclaimed the charge of annexa-

tion tendency,—he flung back the charge with indignation. (Cheers.)

Mr. McDONALD was then allowed to proceed as follows :—Sir, I am delighted to hear these sentiments ; they are sentiments I love to hear. I should have been very much disappointed if Mr. Gamble had given utterance to any others ; they are sentiments which do honour to his head and heart. I am prepared, for one, to repudiate annexation, in the manner that this resolution does, and go in for our connection with Great Britain for an indefinite period of time, until at our full growth we may take our place among the nations of the earth—that is my pride and ambition—that is what I desire to do—to build up this country ; and I tell you that this country is one of the greatest countries on the face of God's earth. I will now read to gentlemen who may not have paid much attention to the subject, what this country is considered to be capable of by one of the first historians of the age, Alison ; and I hope that when gentlemen hear how much we are though of abroad, they will not think we are such a miserable set of people as Mr Gow in made us out to be ; he did it perhaps for the purpose of casting reflections on the Government, but I disclaim such a thing ; I say we are flourishing and doing well. Some few millers and others may say they are not doing well, but I say the country is doing well as a whole. Here is Mr. Alison's description of Canada :

" Canada and the other British possessions in North America, though apparently blessed with fewer physical advantages, contain a nobler race and are evidently reserved for a more lofty destination than the United States. Everything there is in proper keeping for the development of the combined physical and mental energies of man. There are to be found at once, the hardihood of character which conquers difficulty, the severity of climate which stimulates exertion, the natural advantages which reward enterprize. Nature has marked out this country for exalted destinies : for if she has not given it the virgin mould of the basin of the Missouri, or the giant vegetation and prolific sun of the tropics, she has bestowed upon it a vast chain of inland lakes, which fit it one day to become the great channel of commerce between Europe and the interior of America and eastern parts of Asia. The river St. Lawrence, fed by the immense inland seas which separate Canada from the United States, is the great commercial artery of North America. Descending from the distant sources of Kaministiquia and St. Louis, it traverses the solitary Lake Winnipeg, the Lake of the Woods, opens into the boundless expanse of Lake Superior, and after being swelled by the tributary volumes of the Michigan and Huron waves, again contracts into the river and lake of St. Clair ; a second time expands into the broad surface of Lake Erie, from whence it is precipitated by the sublime cataract of Niagara into " wide Ontario's boundless lake," and again contracting finds its way to the sea by the magnificent estuary of the St. Lawrence, through the wooded intricacies of the Thousand Islands.—

*   *   *   *   *

The superficial extent of the British possessions in North America is prodigious, and greatly exceeds that which is subject to the sway of the United States ; it amounts to about 4,000,000 of square geographical miles, or nearly a ninth part of the whole terrestrial surface of the globe "

And again—

" In many of the fundamental particulars which distinguish the United States of America from all other countries of the world, the British Provinces in Canada entirely participate. They have the same boundless extent of unappropriated territory, in some places rich and fertile, in others sterile and unproductive ; the same active and persevering race to subdue it : the same restless spirit of adventure, perpetually urging men into the recesses of the forest in quest of independence ; the same spirit of freedom and enterprize ; the same advantages arising from the powers of knowledge, the habits of civilization, the force of credit, the capacities of industry. Their progress in respect of wealth and population, accordingly, has been nearly at the same rate, at least since in the middle of the last century, they fell under the British dominion, as that of the neighbouring Provinces in the United States ; and b)th have regularly gone on doubling in somewhat less than a quarter of a century—a rate of advance which may be considered as the maximum of colonial increase in the most favourable circumstances, and when largely aided by emigration from the parent state. The total inhabitants of the British possessions in America are now about one million, seven hundred thousand ; but when it is recollected that the natural increase of this number is aided by an immigration annually of from thirty to forty thousand persons in the prime of life from the British islands, which number is rapidly increasing, it may well be imagined that it is destined to become ere long, one of the most powerful states of the new world "

Hear also what he says of the character of this people. " In Upper Canada in particular which now numbers 450000 inhabitants, these sentiments are particularly strong, and the large body of Scottish Highlanders who have settled on its ice-clad wilds, have borne with them from their native mountains the loyal ardour by which their race has been distinguished in every period of England's history. [I am a Highlander myself.— (Laughter.) I am a Highlander in every sense of the word, and so was my father and my mother before me] On every occasion of hazard they have been foremost at the post of honour, and to the patriotic attachment of the inhabitants of that noble Province, the preservation of these magnificent possessions is mainly to be ascribed" (Cheers.) Now, Sir, it is to carry out the idea entertained in that book, that I desire that this colony, instead of being annexed to the U. States, should carry out the evident designs of Providence by becoming a country. Let both parties in this country clear their skirts of annexation, let both Reformers and Conservatives say that with regard to those who advocate annexation, they have neither lot nor part with them, and I say that if the present administration would only take proper views of things, this country might be in a prosperous condition. The first thing they should do would be to send home Lord Elgin, —I almost hate to mention the name of the man : it is gall and wormwood to me, and he never can do any good here Then there is one cause of disunion removed, one complication less ; then people can come forward and say, " you have sent that fellow home, and we will come and consider what can be done for the good of the country " Let them clear their skirts of all annexation ; let them carry out that system which will decrease the expenditure of the country, which they already begin to say they will do—which the League has compelled them to do, but let them have the credit if they will only do it. Let them try to do something through Great Britain to open the markets of the United States to us ; let them try to do something for the good of the country, and the consequence will be, we shall be great and prosperous ; let them carry out

this union—let us become a people, a nation, and whether you are for independence or annexation, we will have the machinery for either the one or the other, for it will be the policy of Great Britain to try and rear up an empire on this continent that will be a sort of check to the gigantic Republic on the south. But, Sir, is there nothing else than money to be considered in this matter ; is there no higher principle at stake than the mere £ s. d. ? I feel deeply humiliated that any person should be obliged to descend to argue this question on the mere ground of £ s. d. ; I think it is to be deplored that there is such a want of public spirit, of patriotism and of loyalty, not to the crown of Great Britain, but loyalty to the country. (Cheers.) I blush to have had to argue on the advantage or disadvantage of annexation Sir, there are people in this country who would rather live on a crust of dry bread under the constitution we live under, than join the United States, and the question must be decided on higher principles than mere £ s. d. Sir, has it come to this, that the people of this country are prepared to sell their birthright for a mess of pottage ; and not for a mess of pottage either, for it is only a promise. Are we to be called upon to give up our share and our inheritance in the glory of Britain—is it come to this, that we are to give up our share in Cressy, Poictiers, all the battles that have been fought on the continent, and in the glory of the crowning triumph of Waterloo—are we to give up our inheritance in the great Statesmen, Poets, and Orators, that have raised the renown of Britain from one end of the world to the other— are we to give up our share in, the immortal Nelson's victories of the Nile, Camperdown, St. Vincent, and Trafalgar ? No ! We are not prepared to do it, and in addition to this, are we prepared to join England's bitterest enemy ? I say no ! Are we prepared to pull down the glorious old flag of England and raise up the stars and stripes—the paltry rag—the gridiron.— (Cheers.) Sir, I shall suppose one of the persons who signed the Montreal Manifesto, hereafter present on an occasion of the Fourth of July in the United States ; we will suppose the Americans are glorifying themselves and abusing Great Britain, and talking about the great independence they achieved, could he look on and enjoy it—could he join in the acclamations that would greet their orator of the day—while this was going on, would not such an individual rather hide his face from the finger of scorn that would be pointed at him as the traitor—the man who sold his country ? (Cheers.) Or would he not rather retire, bearing back his thirty pieces of silver and do as Judas Iscariot did, go and kill himself ? (Cheers) Are we ready, Sir, to allow our children to forget the songs of " Rule Britannia " and " God save the Queen," and teach them in return to lisp " Yankee Doodle."— (Cheers and laughter.) Are we prepared to give up our inheritance in the nation that says, that the moment a slave touches her soil, that moment he is free ; and above all, are we prepared to say that there shall be no Canada for the poor slaves of the south to run to, and escape from the hands of their hard hearted masters ? (Cheers.) Are we prepared to say that on this continent there shall be no refuge for the poor sons of Canaan ? No, we are not. I would tell the annexationist, above all, that there are people in this country who will never submit to be annexed to the people of the United States ; there are people who, if England would consent to give us up and the United States consent to take us in (and they are great hands at that,) would never consent to join the United States ; they would take up the swords which have been lying by rusting since 1813, their children would rally round them and it never could be effected peaceably. Oh, you annexationists that don't desire to fight for annexation, don't lay the flattering unction to your souls, that you ever can get it without fighting ; it will only be got through oceans of blood, and I tell you for one, that rather than consent to it, I would be willing to sacrifice my heart's best blood. I have taken the oath of allegiance, I repeat that oath now, and I say that if I ever forsake that great country— my own country, may Heaven forsake me in my hour of greatest need. (Cheers.)

'Breathes there a man with soul so dead,
Who never to himself has said,
This is my own, my native land.

If there is such a man in this assembly, I don't envy him his feelings. [Mr. McDonald resumed his seat amidst loud cheers both from above and below the bar.]

Mr. GAMBLE said, that one would suppose from the speech of the gentleman opposite, that he and the gentlemen who voted with him were the only gentlemen in this country who were loyal to their Sovereign or felt an interest in the prosperity of their country, and that to them exclusively and peculiarly belonged loyalty and everything attached to it. (Hear, hear.) But the gentleman in his great eagerness to blame those, whom he (Mr. Gamble) could not blame so much, had thought fit to be guilty of the most gross inconsistency (Hear, hear) He had been told in the first place, and the application was so personal that he (Mr. G.) did not pretend to avoid it, that *Punch* had invented a Flourometer, by which you might ascertain the loyalty of a class of people whom he styled annexationists ; he said that when flour was up at 33s. loyalty was up, when it was down at 26s. it was cold, and that when it was down to 22s. it bordered on annexation. By that he meant to insinuate that the loyalty of those gentlemen who were engaged in the flour trade was measured by their pockets ; that was his assertion, that they were so selfish and covetous, so given to the love of gold, that they could not entertain any sentiment of loyalty towards their Sovereign which was not felt in their pockets; and then the learned gentleman went on to say, that these same gentlemen, so covetous, so unwilling to part with their shillings when annexation was the question, cared nothing for the money spent by the troops here; that those people so exceedingly covetous, whose loyalty moved with their flour, up and down, had no regard for their money. He (Mr. G.) would like the

gentleman to reconcile one statement with the other, for they appeared to him to be grossly inconsistent—(hear, hear) –but he would suggest that that expenditure, which so far as it goes, he valued, was by no means to be compared with the same sum invested in any industrial pursuit, and that was one reason why he could not go with his friends in Toronto in thinking the seat of government was such an acquisition ; if the same sum as the government would expend was expended in any industrial pursuit, it would give them far greater prosperity, because the operative before he can spend his five shillings must have made that five shillings into some material by his labour; besides the money spent, you would have the material also. He would ask those gentlemen who claimed so exclusively all the loyalty of the country, whether the interests of this their native or adopted country should not be paramount to the interests of any other country ? Was there any thing inconsistent or extraordinary in that demand ? He (Mr. G) believed that Alison's account of the feeling of the Canadians was a true one. He would himself vouch for its truth he knew the sort of feeling that flowed in his own breast—it had no connection with £ s. d. —it was a chivalrous feeling—it was the old cavalier spirit of an age gone by ; but he could not forget the time when in 1837 he took his rifle in his hand, and looked on his family, thinking that it might be his last look on all that was near and dear to him, and when the property he left behind was in danger of destruction—that was an event which was not easily forgotten ; and when he thought that that power for which he was ready to shed his life's bl od, had turned round and told him that he was a foe to the liberties of his country, (great cheering), and when ministers of the Crown had styled him and the gallant men who turned out at the same time to keep this Province a dependency of the British Crown, "traitors," when his loyalty had been called "spurious loyalty," (cheers) when the government prints in Great Britain turned round on those individuals, whom the ever-varying policy of Great Britain had reduced to poverty, and called them bankrupts, the feelings that were once here (laying his hand on his heart) were not still to be found there, although he trusted they were not entirely forgotten . Great cheering.) And with regard to this " self," he maintained that mankind in general are intensely selfish (Hear, hear) Of the many springs of human action, self and the love of approbation are two of the strongest of these motives. (Hear, hear.) It was the love of approbation that placed Mr. McDonald on his feet and induced him to make the speech they had heard This love of approbation actuates man in infancy from the first perception of the mother's smile, and it clings to him in the last stages of human existence. when he hopes that his children will honour his memory. (Hear, hear.) The gentleman's inconsistency did not end with the flourometer; he next said he hoped the time would come when we should be a nation, and stand on our own legs, meaning by that that we should be independent; he taxed others with disloyalty and disregard of their allegiance, and yet, according to his own showing, it was only a question of degree or time, only some people think the time has already come, and he thinks it *will* come but has not come; here then was another inconsistency. (Cheers.) For his (Mr. Gamble's) part, he was quite sick of hearing about the "old flag", and "glory," and all that sort of thing, that was not the way in which the annexationists should be answered—their reasonings should be met by reasonings, and their arguments by sound arguments He was not going to enter into the question now, but he would like to know if it was any reply to those gentlemen who put forth their arguments on paper and challenged an answer, for Mr. McDonald to tell them that he was the son of a Highlander, and that his mother was the *son of a Highlander.* (Roars of laughter, amidst which Mr. Gamble corrected the bull.) He would put it to the learned gentleman whether he furthered the cause in which he seemed so zealous, by any argument of that description? (Cheers.) The next and last thing he would advert to, was the manner in which Mr. McDonald had deprecated their covetousness and selfishness, and this sort of £ s. d. loyalty—

Mr. McDonald asked why Mr. Gamble spoke of "us" and "our," if he was not an annexationist?

Mr. Gamble did so because he had been alluded to by name. With regard to the £ s. d. loyalty, it had been well remarked by Mr. Gowan, that the home government itself had put it as a matter of pounds, shillings and pence, although that was not the principle that formerly governed us in this country.

Mr. Mack said that it was impossible for him or any one else to treat the question now before the chair in anything like a serious manner. He had felt for Mr. McDonald, at the unfortunate position in which he had been placed; he had been obliged to create an imaginary opposition, like the man who used to wash his his hands with fancied soap and an imaginary basin of water. He first tried to constitute into an opposition, those who spoke last night in favour of the elective principle; but knowing they were all of one opinion on this question, he must have felt like the gentleman using the imaginary basin. He believed they were all of one opinion on the question of annexation, and he was really tired of hearing all these expressions about loyalty; their loyalty ought to be well understood; there was no need of maintaining it except in stirring times—it should, like the honour of a man or the virtue of a woman, never be mentioned by himself or herself. (Cheers.) His loyalty was like that of gentlemen opposite, although he had never threatened to die for it (cheers and laughter); and he thought the resolution, and the remarks made in support of it, quite uncalled for. The participators in the Montreal manifesto were not present to defend themselves, and it was quite

useless raising up men of straw and knocking them down again, for the purpose of giving vent to expressions of loyalty. (Hear, hear.) They might just as well resolve that the breakfast they had eaten that morning was necessary for their bodily health; it was equally undeniable. He again protested against their accusations of disloyalty. He challenged his venerable friend Colonel Playfair to feel more loyalty at heart than he (Mr. Mack) did; and perhaps if it came to the struggle, he too might be ready to die for his loyalty. But there was no danger of such a struggle: the danger to be apprehended was from the cold scorn of the English government, and the policy of the Manchester school, the Cobdenites and the Greyites; and in case of this colony being alienated from Great Britain—not through actual misgovernment, but owing to indifference towards the colonies—the difference between him (Mr. Mack) and his venerable friend (Col. Playfair) would be this: the latter would have his sons and daughters and grandchildren to bind him to the soil by the tenderest ties—he would live only under the vine that he had planted, although he might weep and be sorrowful to see the strange flag waving over him; but he (Mr. Mack) had no such ties to bind him to Canada—he had but the profession which had been so much sneered at, but of which he had never been ashamed; he could not continue here—he should have to go home; and, as he was not likely, by any conduct he had pursued here, to have sufficient interest with the Whig government to obtain employment even in breaking stones by the way-side, he should have to get a board and chalk upon it—"Pity, good Christians, a poor devil who was too loyal for Canada!"

[Mr. Mack resumed his seat, amidst much cheering and laughter.]

Mr. Hamilton moved, in amendment—

"That it is wholly inexpedient to discuss the question of Annexation at this Convention, the loyalty of whose members cannot be questioned, and amongst whom, as a body, there is found no individual to advocate any such obnoxious principle."

He hoped that now the exuberance of their loyalty had passed off, the gentlemen would withdraw the resolution. As far as his experience went, he never knew anything to be wrung from the British, or any other government, except by a firm and manly expression of opinion. It was this which obtained Catholic emancipation in 1829, and indeed he had never known a man or a government to yield anything to people who said they did not want it, and he believed that the only possible advantage in mooting the question of annexation was this: that England should see from the proceedings of this large assembly of independent men, representing an important portion of the community, that unless the evils under which this community suffers are redressed, there is no saying how far those men may be hurried unwillingly into the arms of annexation. That was the use he wished to make of the question of annexation, and he would not like to see it put down by the Convention; he would like them to meet the question like men. and not to put forward the blood-red cross of England, and the flag of Eng -

land, and all that species of thing ; and he could tell those gentlemen who boasted of their loyalty that they could not carry that feeling into the hearts of the farmer and the men who have to eat their bread in the sweat of their brows ; he could tell those gentlemen more, that there was amongst the farmers of this country a belief that they must get rid of these feelings. Why he (Mr. D.) alone, out of his small crop, on which he was not dependent for a living, lost by the recent policy of Great Britain, $150 ; he lost that sum by taking his crop to St. Catharines instead of to Lewiston, and would any body tell him that the farmers of the country, who are dependent on their crops for a livelihood, would long endure this state of things, without thinking of a change ? he believed not ; he did not believe that all the flags you could exhibit to them, or all the swords and muskets either, would prevent this progressive feeling from developing itself ; it might come gradually, but in this as in every other country, £ s. d. would ultimately prevail. He contended that they had not met there to talk about the glorious flag which every body venerated, there was no one present who wanted to pull it down, but they were met to find out the causes that were working at the foundation of it, and which if not stopped must necessarily destroy it. Those knew nothing of the feelings of the agricultural population, who did not know that the question is now being asked, "why is it my wheat is not as valuable on this side of line 45, as on the other ?" This question was growing in interest, and he had even heard amongst the statesmen of England, the question of expediency urged. That was the excuse for Catholic emancipation and the Reform Bill, when they jumped Jim Crow. If this resolution were carried, the effect would be, that it would be supposed that no matter what England did, we would still remain perfectly loyal. Now although he thought it a great waste of time to make speeches about loyalty, as there were no annexationists in the Convention, still he did not think that they would forget the insult which had been cast upon the men who turned out in 1837-8, to put down the rebellion, by rewarding those who rebelled ; he did not think that they should allow Lord Elgin, or any other man, to trample on them. He had heard the oath of allegiance alluded to, he too had taken that oath against all treason and conspiracy, and, might the day that found him engaged in treason and conspiracy find him in his grave ; but he would still claim to exercise the Constitutional right to alter the fundamental principles of the Constitution when circumstances required it. He thought that the question of annexation had been dragged in unnecessarily, and that the passage of this resolution would destroy the effect of their previous proceedings in England, and he would therefore move the amendment.

After some remarks from Colonels Fraser and Playfair,

Mr. JOHN DUGGAN regretted that the subject had been introduced, as it was quite unnecessary, but they could not now reject the resolution without a danger of their motives being misunderstood by the country. He therefore hoped the amendment would be withdrawn.

Mr. GEORGE DUGGAN, as seconder of the amendment, could never consent to withdraw it ; he considered the proposition contained in the resolution utter nonsense ; they had been convened together to apply a remedy to the evils under which the country groans. One day they were talking about England's tyranny and injustice, and the rewarding of rebels, and the next talking about their attachment to the English government. Was the payment of rebels the way to attach the people of this country to England—to strengthen the ties that bind us together—to excite our love and admiration ? (Question, question.) He supported the amendment because he did not think they were called on to trumpet forth their loyalty, but to apply remedies to the evils that are weighing down the energies of the country.

After a few words from Mr. Aikman the amendment was rejected and the resolution carried.

WEDNESDAY, Nov. 7, 10 o'clock A. M.

The Convention met this morning, and after a conversational discussion relative to some matters of routine, which will be found amongst the printed proceedings, a vote of thanks to the President was passed amidst loud cheers, and briefly acknowledged.

Mr. LANGTON then rose and said that after the division on the question of elective institutions, the minority felt that the question would not rest there, and they therefore agreed to remain till the close of the Convention and take part in the proceedings, on the understanding that the Convention should then be dissolved and the matter referred to their constituents for the purpose of settling the matter in dispute.— He would therefore move, seconded by Mr. Gamble :

That whereas a difference has arisen in this Convention upon the question of elective institutions, and whereas, the majority of the members present have declared that the Legislative Council should continue to be appointed by the Crown, subject to limitation as to number, and not be elected by the people as contended for by the minority, and this Convention having disposed of the other business brought before it : Be it therefore resolved, that this Convention be now adjourned, to a day to be hereafter named by the Central Committee, with a view to the several branches of the British American League pronouncing their opinion, and instructing their delegates upon the question of the concession of elective institutions to Canada, as an appendage to the British Crown, and that the several branches do make a return to the Secretary of the Central Society Toronto, of the delegates whom they may appoint, on or before the 1st day of January next.

Which was carried unanimously.

The Convention was then adjourned.

Lightning Source UK Ltd.
Milton Keynes UK
UKHW021609110119
335365UK00008B/723/P